TRiO

WORKS

40 Leadership Activities
&
Team-Building Initiatives
for TRiO Groups

Ryan Eller & Jerrod Murr
Paradigm Shift

This book is dedicated to all the TRiO professionals who are doing what is necessary to change the world.

Table of Contents

TRiO Works - Our Personal Case Study   8

Pool Party Process   10

TRiO Works Basic Rules   14

TRiO Works Constants   16

The User Guide   19

Activities   22

     Candy Factory   22

     Careeragories   24

     College Admissions Rank 'Em   27

     Count the Beans   30

     Design by 3   32

     Diversity Cards   34

     Draw Yourself   41

     Dream Catcher   43

     Fill the Basket   46

     Financial Aid Matching   50

     Gallery Walk   53

     Gridwalk   54

     Head, Heart, Hands   57

     Hey You!   58

     Human Mastermind   59

     Joboo   61

     Landmarks   64

Table of Contents

Leader vs. Leader	66
Likert Scale	68
Make a Shake	69
Name Etymology	70
One Word Whip	71
Paint Swatches	72
Pit	73
Pitfall	75
Plan That Mine	78
Plumber Pete	80
Popcorn	81
Post an Emotion	84
Post-It Party	85
Quadrants	86
Saying Goodbye	89
Show Me The Money	90
SMART Goal Paper Fold	91
Snakes	94
Take a Stand	97
Talking Toys	99
Tongue in Cheek	100
Web of Names	101
You Get a Prize	102

Table of Contents

Lesson Plans   103

     Career Connections   105

     College Admissions   106

     Communication Skills   107

     Community Learning   108

     Decision Making   109

     Diversity Awareness   110

     Financial Aid   111

     Goal Setting   112

     High School Success   113

     Leadership   114

     Managing Money   115

     Non-Verbal Speech   116

     Planning Dreams   117

     SMART Goals   118

     Time Management   119

     Trust Your Strengths   120

Paradigm Shift   121

Workshops   122

EmotiCARDS   127

EmotiCARDS Activity Guide   128

Authors   129

Notes   130

TRiO Works - My Personal Case Study

It was my first day on the job and we might have had better engagement with the students if we were selling life insurance. It was the Fall of 2006 and I was a bright-eyed guidance counselor for Educational Talent Search who was ready to change the world. However, to the seniors in the room, this presentation on financial aid was as interesting as evidence of insurability and disclosure statements.

It was in that moment that I knew we needed to spice up our presentations and workshops. I wanted to find a way to present our core objectives - college readiness, high school success, career planning, financial aid - to students in a way that was not only engaging, but helped create substantial change in their lives.

I started a journey. I wanted to learn every way in which I could engage our participants. The director of our ETS program, Diane Walker, was a huge believer in experiential education...or learning by doing. She was constantly encouraging us to develop new ideas for workshops that would both meet the needs of our students and our program.

We went to trainings, workshops, and seminars on how to present our material experientially. We tried some things that worked...and some things that did not. I presented our new material at a "Best Practices" session at the SWASAP conference. The participants of the session asked for more the following year...so I continued learning.

TRiO Works

I found that the more we encouraged our students to become involved with our materials, the better the results. I joined with other TRiO professionals and leadership facilitators, like Jerrod Murr, who were on a mission to change lives. We started gaining more knowledge, more experience, and more results.

This is my history and this is why I wrote this book. I spent seven years in TRiO and have spent the last few years consulting with TRiO programs across the country. TRiO programs that are looking for quality educational initiatives and team-building activities to make a difference with their groups.

Quite frankly, there are not a tremendous amount of quality educational-based activity books. Fortunately, I have worked with Jerrod Murr and other facilitators for some time now, and know quite a few relevant activities. Jerrod and I bring a knowledge of experiential education that is completely underutilized in TRiO.

We have worked with groups of all sizes in a variety of sectors. We have a wealth of icebreakers, name games, and leadership initiatives that we use with groups for years. We paired new, engaging games with deep, educational lessons to create the activities for this book.

We work with students all over the world. We have seen the power of these activities to connect with students. We bring this experience to a usable format for leaders. We wrote this book for TRiO because we know TRiO Works.

- Ryan Eller

Pool Party Process

How to Get the Most Out of This Book

This book is based upon experiential learning. Experiential learning is the process of making meaning from direct experience, i.e., "learning from experience."

Aristotle once said, "For the things we have to learn before we can do them, we learn by doing them." To best achieve this, you must build trust with your group. Like swimming, you can't just jump in deep freezing water, and expect to have a wonderful day. You have to work your way toward deeper levels of learning, a process we affectionately call "The Pool Party Process."

The Pool Party Process aids facilitators and group leaders of all experience levels to create substantial change during their programs. We have separated the Pool Party Process into four sequential steps:

1. Break the Ice
2. Warm the Water
3. Swim
4. Towel Off

In our research on how to engage participants, we found the best way to create substantial change was to first break down the social barriers within a group (Break the Ice) and then to build rapport and community (Warm the Water). Once we developed a relationship with our participants, we could then ask them to learn about our curriculum (Swim). Finally, we would make sure everyone understood the information before leaving (Towel Off).

The Pool Party Process

Break The Ice

Breaking the ice is the first step to a successful lesson. This is simply connecting with your group and allowing the group to connect with each other. Members of any group must be comfortable, and have an established level of trust with each other in order to better learn. This can be achieved through basic introductions, name games, or classic icebreakers we have played in TRiO for years.

Generally, competitive games are not advised as icebreakers. They tend to divide a group, and are often exclusive. The goals of an icebreaker are the opposite, unity and inclusion. The goal of Breaking the Ice is letting group members know this is a safe group where they can grow and be themselves.

Warm the Water

After the ice has been broken, you should continue by warming the water. This is really about building a rapport with your group. Warming the water is a continuation of breaking the ice, and can be achieved in similar ways. The best Warm the Water activities are ones that help the group create agreements about the social norms within the group.

You, as the facilitator, must read the group and determine what type of activity is best for the group to develop social norms. If many in the group are new to each other, several name games would be appropriate. If the group already knows each other by name, a fun energizer may work wonders. In some cases, asking the group to develop rules and guidelines to follow may be necessary.

The goal here is to have fun and make the group feel comfortable enough to share. This is achieved through play, laughter, and establishing common bonds.

Swim

The ice is broken and the water is warm. Now, it's time to swim! Swimming is the heart of your lesson, and what most people immediately think of in terms of curriculum.

As a TRiO program, you know you absolutely need to talk about financial literacy or student loans. The activities in this book were specifically designed to help you deliver your curriculum.

These activities are purposed as learning devices. Lead your participants through these activities so they can grow from the activity itself. Some activities are more challenging than others, and groups will respond to activities differently. All of that is ok. Just like swimming, there are many ways to do it.

Pool Party Process

Towel Off

Most people think you are finished when your main activity is finished. Not so. That's like swimming, and going home wet! You must process the needs of your group to find your best results.

Processing can simple, such as asking what everyone learned from an activity. It can be more complex like having a group discuss in depth or completing a new activity as a debriefing exercise.

Here's what's important. Allow group members to express how they felt and what they learned. Encourage them to discuss or write down what action steps they need to take with this new information.

You can think in terms of three questions. What actually happened in the activity (i.e. We had to get the ball across the line, and it was difficult)? How did it feel during the activity (i.e. Frustrating because no one would listen)? What can we learn going forward from this activity (i.e. we should take time to listen to each other)?

The "Questions for Discussion" listed with each activity in this book are designed to process, or "Towel Off," the group. The "Facilitators Notes" component of each activity can be used in conjunction with these questions, or as a stand-alone processing opportunity from the activity.

Basic Rules

TRiO Works Basic Rules

Circle Up

The easiest way to introduce an activity from this book is to gather the participants into a circle. Circles allow all the participants to see each other and create a sense of equality within a group. No one stands before or above anyone else in a circle, not even the facilitator. Be sure to circle up the group as much as you can, whether it is in a classroom, gym, field or open room.

Break the Group Up

Some of these activities will work in large groups, but not all of them will. The best group size for the majority of these activities is between 15-20 people. If you find that you are in a group much larger than that, break the group up into smaller groups and have them rotate when sequencing into a new activity. This assures that the participants will not only interact with the people in their small group, but that they will have opportunities to meet other people as well!

Take Time to Make it Timed

Making the activity a timed event creates a completely new variation to any activity, and changes the dynamics of the group. Feel free to add this new element to any activity that does not already have timing as a variation.

Basic Rules

Practice Makes Perfect

There is no better way to improve as a facilitator then through trial and error. Try out these activities with your family, your friends, and your closest group. Regardless of how well you know the group, you will discover new things about the participants.

Find the ones you love and try new variations and techniques. Introduce new stories and new variations that fit the personality of your group.

Remember: You can read about swimming, watch people swim, and learn from swimming masters, but you will not become a swimmer until you get in the pool. The same is true for these activities. Try them out, get used to leading a group, and these activities will truly open up your options as a facilitator.

Go Deeper

Many of these activities are often silly, fun and high energy, however they are also a great way to get participants to talk about themselves. Often we are too shy or guarded to delve into our personal lives, and these initiatives are an easy way to get our participants to open up and become more informal within a group. This will help groups to work more fluently and successfully in future situations that can become complicated or frustrating.

Constants

TRiO Works Constants

Many of the following activities differ greatly on energy level, age range and participant engagement. Regardless there are several "constants" with the activities that do not change regardless of initiative, location, or age. As a facilitator it is your responsibility to make sure these constants are followed by each participant and each different group.

Constant #1: Be positive!

Our good friend Mark Collard always says, "If it ain't fun, it ain't worth doing!" These activities should be fun and allow participants to open up to a group in a new and entertaining way.

It is important that all participants feel comfortable and welcome as they act silly, run around or share something personal. As the facilitator, you must always be positive and create an atmosphere that assures all participants that negativity, snickering or bullying is never an option.

Feel free to create these guidelines before you even get started, inviting the group to stay positive and encouraging throughout the entire day! Staying firm and positive as a facilitator will develop a sense of unity and togetherness that will allow all the participants to open up in their own personal way.

Constants

Constant #2: Be the example.

As the facilitator, you are going to ask your participants to do some crazy and wacky activities. You must always be willing to go first to show the group how crazy and wacky they can be!

Have fun, get into it, and show the participants that they can have fun too. Say your name in a funny accent, do a silly dance or create an imaginative motion for your name even if you know you will make a fool of yourself.

The participants will appreciate your initiative, your enthusiasm and your sense of humor and will more than likely be willing to do the same. Regardless of how the activity goes, everyone knows you are going to be participating with them and that you are having fun while doing it!

Constant #3: Be loud and clear.

Encourage each participant to speak up and share clearly and proudly. This teaches participants regardless of age or gender to be proud of who they are, and will create a sense of confidence within the group.

There is no reason to yell, but there is no reason to whisper either. Nothing will stop an activity in its tracks like a facilitator speaking so softly that no one can hear them! Stay positive and lead by example as a facilitator by speaking clearly and loudly to the group when you are explaining the rules and actions of the activities.

Constant #4: Be inclusive.

Whenever any group comes together, there can often be one or two people who would rather be eating dirt or tarring roofs than be with the group. It is important that everyone participates with every activity.

If you can get everyone involved early in the process while Breaking the Ice, chances are good that the entire group will stay engaged for the rest of the day's activities.

Be sure to creative an environment the beginning of the day where everyone wants to participate. Encourage the group to be inclusive to make sure everyone participates. It will be easier for you as a facilitator if the group's members are encouraging everyone to join in on the fun name games!

Constant #5: Be fun to have fun.

These activities are meant for the participants to have fun and interact within a group. Whether the initiative is high energy or low energy, it is important that group laughs, has fun and develops a sense of camaraderie.

As a facilitator make sure to gauge the group's "fun level" throughout the activities to make sure they are still engaged. Usually if a group is not engaged in the activity, they need to go back a few steps in the Pool Party Process. The activities in this book create new opportunities for a group to grow and allow participants to be creative, entertaining, and unique.

The User Guide

There are 40 different activities and initiatives in this book. The activities range from highly interactive and fun to low-key and involved. We have organized the instructions within the activities to be simple and consistent so you can lead them effectively.

Activities in this book are listed alphabetically and provide simple sections that help you better understand how to facilitate each activity.

Short Description

Included at the top of each page is a short description of the activity and how it could be useful for a TRiO program.

Number of Participants

The ideal size of the group for the activity. This number is suggested, however feel free to try variations of the activity to meet the needs of you group. Also, don't hesitate to split your group into smaller groups if necessary.

Time

The recommend amount of time to lead the activity (times are approximate and can be changed to fit the needs of your group).

The User Guide

Activity Level

Describes the activity level of the activity as either Low, Moderate, or High. Of course, you will determine the pace in which the activity is facilitated, but most High Energy activities are often more physically demanding. Be aware of the abilities of your group before asking them to take part in a High Energy activity.

Pool Party

This section details which step of the Pool Party Process the activity usually falls under. Check the variations to see how it could be facilitated in another step.

Props

Many of the activities in this book require no additional materials, but this section will explain what materials you will need to round up.

Set Up

Explains how to set up the room or facility for the activity.

Objective

Brief description that explains the goals and objective of activity. This will be what the group will be trying to achieve.

The User Guide

Step by Step

This is the "How-To" section of the activity. It includes any relevant information that would be helpful before introducing the activity and step-by-step instructions for the actual facilitation of the activity.

Questions for Discussion

At the end of each activity, we have suggested a handful of questions to help your participants "Towel Off." These are not the only questions you can ask your group. We encourage you to ask questions that are customized to your group.

Facilitator Notes

Recommendations for facilitating the activity, tips for beginners, and tools to discuss the activity's relevance.

Pool Party Variations

Sample ways to facilitate the activity in a different capacity. Most activities can be used to Break the Ice, Warm the Water, Swim, and Towel Off.

TRiO Specific Variations

Some activities work best for ETS, some for McNair. These activities are merely a framework on how facilitate. What makes TRiO special is when the group facilitator uses creativity to best fit the needs of the participants.

Candy Factory

Candy Factory is an interactive brainstorming activity that helps participants understand the scale of job opportunities in a particular area.

Number of Participants: 2-25
Time: 20-25 minutes
Activity Level: Low
Pool Party: Swim
Props: Dry Erase Board or Large Butcher Paper, Markers, Candy

Set Up:
Draw a circle in the middle of the dry erase board. Inside of the circle write the word, "Candy Factory."

Objective:
To brainstorm as many careers possible that would be found at a candy factory.

Step by Step:
1. Encourage the group to brainstorm careers that would be found at a candy factory.
2. Draw a new line from the Candy Factory circle as they brainstorm different areas within the factory - such as manufacturing, administration, production, etc. Each time the group comes up with a new job, circle the word and keep brainstorming.
3. Try to come up with as many specific careers within each area. When a participant thinks of a career, give them a piece of candy!

"Leadership and learning are indispensable to each other." - JFK

Candy Factory

Questions for Discussion:
- What careers on the board do you find most interesting?

- Find a career. What kind of education or training would be required to have this career?

- Does anyone in your family have one of the careers on the board? What is that career like?

Facilitator Notes:
If the participants are stalling on careers, feel free to brainstorm with them or help them along. It sometimes helps to create the first three or four bubbles to show the participants how to start brainstorming.

Pool Party Variations:
1. **Swim:** Use a different career to brainstorm - such as a hospital, university, or sports team.

2. **Towel Off:** Use Candy Factory as a processing tool after another activity. Ask the participants to share the different experiences they observed. Encourage the group to brainstorm new ideas as they process.

TRiO Specific Variations:
1. **SSS, EOC, & VUB**- Candy Factory takes a new twist with adults. Many of the participants have had several jobs. Ask them to start with a category and then share the specifics of the job, such as salary, education required, etc.

"Life has no remote. Get up and change it yourself." - Unknown

Careeragories

Careeragories is based off of the popular game Scattergories in which the players try to guess as many jobs that start with the letter chosen. Use this as an opportunity to introduce careers to your group.

Number of Participants: 8-25
Time: 10-15 minutes
Activity Level: Low
Pool Party: Warm the Water
Props: Scattergories Die (If you don't have one, just pick letters out of a hat), Careeragories Game Sheet You can download a PDF copy of the Careeragories sheet at myparadigmshift.org/careeragories.

Set Up:
Give every participant a Careeragories Game Sheet and explain the rules.

Objective:
To brainstorm as many careers possible that start with the letter rolled by the facilitator

Step by Step:
1. Roll a 20-sided letter die to determine the first letter used. The timer is set for up to three minutes.
2. In the time allotted, each player must attempt to think of and write down, in the first column on the pad, a job that starts with the rolled letter.
3. All players stop writing when the timer is finished. Following the list, each player, in turn, reads their answer for each category.

"Example is leadership." - Albert Schweitzer

Careeragories

Step by Step:

4. Players score zero points for an answer that duplicates another answer in that round, and one point for an answer no other player has given.

5. Acceptable answers that are proper nouns using alliteration score one point for each word using the letter.

6. The dice is rolled again (and re-rolled if the same letter as the previous round is duplicated), and the second round starts.

Questions for Discussion:

• How hard was it to come up with different careers while under pressure?

• Do any of these careers sound interesting to you? What do you know about those careers?

Facilitator Notes:

We have always used this activity as a way to introduce careers. If we have time we will follow it up with Candy Factory (pg. 22) or an in-depth conversation about career options.

Pool Party Variations:

1. **Break the Ice** - In large groups, use this as an activity to learn names. Give more time but allow players to find names that start with the letter.

2. **Swim** - Split the group into teams and make it a competition. See if the group can think of more careers together than they did individually.

"The book you don't read won't help." - Jim Rohn

Careeragories

Instructions: Come up with as many careers as possible that start with the same letter that was rolled by the instructor. Be as creative as possible! You have two minutes. GO!

1._____	1._____
2._____	2._____
3._____	3._____
4._____	4._____
5._____	5._____
6._____	6._____
7._____	7._____
8._____	8._____
9._____	9._____
10._____	10._____
11._____	11._____
12._____	12._____
13._____	13._____
14._____	14._____

College Rank 'Em

Ever wondered what your participants thought was the most important reason for picking a college? College Admissions Rank 'Em will start the conversation amongst students about the different reasons for deciding on a future college.

Number of Participants: 5-15
Time: 15-45 minutes (depends on how many are in the group, different personalities, etc.)
Activity Level: Low
Pool Party: Swim
Props: Type of a list of factors that any student would consider when choosing post-secondary education. Place each term on a single piece of paper or at least a half sheet of paper. It helps to have each term on their own paper so that the participants can move them around and actually rank them on the floor or table.

Set Up:
Simply place the factors on the floor or on a table so each participant can see the different words.

Objective:
To rank the reason to pick a college from most important to least important as an entire group.

Step by Step:
1. The rules for this activity are very simple: the group must come to a consensus and rank all the college admission factors from most important to least important.

"Leadership does not depend on being right." - Ivan Illich

College Rank 'Em

Questions for Discussion:

- Why did you decide on these final rankings?

- Did anyone compromise for the sake of the group?

- Were there times when you felt passionate about a particular card?

- If you did this by yourself, would you have had a different outcome?

Facilitator Notes:

It is often hard for the group to come to a consensus, and it is more important that they begin talking about these factors than if they come to an actual consensus. Feel free to put a time limit on this activity to keep the activity from lasting several hours!

Use your experience as a professional to help guide them after the activity to the most important factors in their own individual college admissions decision.

Pool Party Variations:

1. **Swim -** Instead of printing the cards ahead of time, encourage a brainstorming session for the participants. They may come up with factors you hadn't thought of, or they may become passionate for the ideas they generated, which hopefully will create more conversation. Encourage the group to use their resources to find more college admission choices.

"Character is much easier kept than recovered." Thomas Paine

College Rank 'Em

Pool Party Variations

2. **Swim** - Have the participants view the factors and then write their own rankings on a piece of paper. They can then share their list to the group and explain why they ranked them.

TRiO Specific Variations:

1. **SSS** - This activity isn't related to just college admissions. Place whatever words you feel need to be discussed on the cards to create dynamic conversations. Have the group rank different careers, graduate schools, or types of loans.

College Admission Factors:

Price
Location
Size
Type (Private or Public)
Academic Rigor
Campus Life
Campus Aesthetics
Your Friends Go There
Your Family
Majors Offered
Athletics
Greek Life
Setting (Urban, Suburban or Rural)
Admissions Criteria
Housing Options
Religious Affiliation

"If there is no action, you haven't truly decided." - Tony Robbins

Count the Beans

Count the Beans shows your group that the collective is greater than the individual. The participants guess how many beans are in a jar and then collaborate with other participants to get the closest guess.

Number of Participants: 10 or More
Time: 15-25 minutes
Activity Level: Low
Pool Party: Swim
Props: Glass Jar Full of Pinto Beans, Paper, Writing Utensils

Set Up:

Empty a bag of pinto beans into a glass jar with a lid. It is very important that the facilitator actually counts the number of beans in the jar for the integrity of the activity.

Objective:

To try and guess the number of beans in the jar.

Step by Step:

1. Place a jar of pinto beans in the middle of the floor, and hand each participant a piece of paper and a writing utensil.
2. Ask everyone to write their name at the top of their paper, and put Round 1, 2, 3, and 4 in the consequent rows.
3. For Round 1, give enough time for each participant to put some deep thought into the process and guess individually how many beans are in the jar.

"Life has no limitations, except the ones you make." -Les Brown

Count the Beans

Step by Step:

4. In Round 2, participants partner up and review guesses. The two then try to come up a group guess.

5. In Round 3, the two participants join another group of two and compare guesses. They then try to come up with a group guess.

6. In Round 4, the entire group discusses their guesses, and comes up with one large group guess. Eventually the facilitator reveals the answer and determines how close the group was to the actual answer.

Questions for Discussion:

• Did your number change during the rounds? Which round were you the closest?

• Did you stand your ground or go with the group? Do you ever find yourself doing that in groups at school or work?

• What other scenarios do you find better results in a group than you do individually?

Facilitator Notes:

Allow enough time and space for the different groups, but set a time limit according to your needs. Sometimes a small group will be engaged in spirited discussion, and some will come to a guess quickly, either way you are getting the groups to interact together.

"We tend to live up to our expectations." - E. Nightingale

Design by 3

An activity that describes the differences in several types of communication. The group must try to pass along a symbol or shape from the back of the line to the front of the line without looking at the original image.

Number of Participants: 3 or More
Time: 10-20 minutes
Activity Level: Low
Pool Party: Swim
Props: Paper, Writing Utensils

Set Up:
Organize the groups into teams of three. Ask them to stand or sit in a single-file line and face the same direction.

Objective:
For the group to successfully draw an image (a stop sign, house, trapezoid, etc.) closest to the original.

Step by Step:
1. Give the person at the back of the line one of the note cards. This person draws the symbol, shape, or image on the back of the person in front of them with their finger.
2. The person in the middle of the line describes the symbol, shape, or image to the person in the front of the line.
3. The person in the front of the line then draws the symbol, shape, or image on their piece of paper.

"A man has to have goals - for a day, for a lifetime" - Ted Williams

Design by 3

Step by Step:

4. The participants cannot ask questions to the others in the line.

5. When the group thinks they are done, they compare the drawing to the original note card.

6. Rotate after each round so all three people can experience the different roles.

Questions for Discussion:

• How does non-verbal communication matter in this activity?

• Do you find yourself trying to explain things but people understand them differently? How do you react when this happens?

• How does information pass from one person to another in your life? What can you do to improve your communication?

Facilitator Note:

Obviously there are touch boundaries being violated during this activity. Be aware of your group and don't ask people to participate if they are not ready. A variation is to eliminate the touching aspect and ask the three to spread information verbally.

Pool Party Variation:

1. **Towel Off** - Ask the group to draw their emotions after an activity or event and then continue the activity as described above.

"Chase your passion, not your pension". -Denis Waitley

Diversity Cards

This activity is perfect for a facilitator who wants to discuss cultural diversity, written and unwritten rules in society, and social norms within a group.

Number of Participants: 16-32
Time: 10-15 minutes
Activity Level: Low
Pool Party: Swim
Props: 4 Decks of playing cards and different instructions for each table (see below)

Set Up:

Four tables with different instructions and a deck of cards for each table. Be sure to not let the participants read or see the rules until the activity is started and the participants have taken their seats.

Objective:

To win the card game and move to the next table.

Step-By-Step:

1. Tell the group that this is a non-talking activity and they should try to stay silent until the entire activity is over. The only time that the group should talk is at the very beginning of the activity when the participants read the rules.
2. Ask the participants to read the instructions at their table and make sure that each participant understands the rules at their table, but they can not ask the other tables for help or clarification.

"Mistakes are the portals of discovery." - James Joyce

Diversity Cards

Step-By-Step:

3. After the rules have been read and discussed, the group can not talk until the end of the activity, and the facilitator removes the rules from each table.

4. The participants play the game according to the rules on their table.

5. When all four groups have finished gameplay, the facilitator will say rotate, and the winners at the individual tables will rotate in a clockwise direction to the next table.

6. Continue play for several rounds.

Questions for Discussion:

- What were the differences at the individual tables?

- Did any of the participants who didn't win know that the rules changed at each table? If not, how did the new members of the group act during the hands?

- What did any of the winners think when they moved to a table with different rules?

- Did any participants get upset or frustrated when another participant thought they had won because of the their previous tables rules?

- How do other cultures around the world view some of the things we do that are social norms?

- Have any participants traveled around the world and noticed cultural differences from the USA?

"To do two things at once is to do neither." -Publilius Syrus

Diversity Cards

Facilitator Notes

If each table follows the rules, the winner will move to the next table which has completely different rules than the previous table. This will create chaos, confusion and misunderstandings to the new group members.

More often than not, someone at the table who did not win will gladly tell the new member how wrong he/she is when they think they have won the hand (non-verbally of course). The new member will be very confused when another participant wins the hand with a 2 of Diamonds instead of an Ace of Spades.

I typically ask the participants to think about the different "cultures" at each table, and if the winners or the participants at the tables had different perspectives of how the activity went.

On the following pages you will find the different instructions for Diversity Cards. You can also download printable and shareable instructions for Diversity Cards at www.myparadigmshift.org/diversitycards.

Pool Party Variations:

1. **Break the Ice:** Play this game just for fun. Sometimes the greatest way to break social barriers in the group is to play an activity with fun as the objective.

"Miracles happen to those who believe in them." - B. Berenson

Diversity Cards

Table #1

1. This is a no talking game!
2. Each player gets an equal number of cards. Discard the extra cards. Place your cards in a pile face-down in front of you. When the facilitator says "Go," turn over the top card to be played with the group (like the card game Spades).
3. Spades trump or defeat all other cards.
4. If a person plays a spade, it wins. If two or more people play spades, the highest spade wins.
5. Ace high to 2 low (the highest card wins).
6. The best card in the deck is the Ace of Spades
7. If no Spade is played, the highest card played wins
8. If there is a tie – the tied players play again to determine the winner
9. At the end of the rounds the participant that collects the most number of cards wins the game at this table.
10. When there is a winner, he/she must move to Table #2 to continue playing when all other tables have finished playing.

Diversity Cards

Table #2

1. This is a no talking game!
2. Each player gets an equal number of cards. Discard the extra cards. Place your cards in a pile face-down in front of you. When the facilitator says go, turn over the top card to be played with the group (like the card game Spades).
3. Hearts trump all other cards.
4. If a person plays a heart, it wins. If two or more people play hearts, the highest heart wins.
5. Ace high to 2 low (the highest card wins).
6. The best card in the deck is the Ace of Hearts.
7. If no Heart is played, the highest card played wins.
8. If there is a tie - the tied players play again to determine the winner.
9. At the end of the rounds the participant that collects the most number of cards wins the game at this table.
10. When there is a winner, he/she must move to Table #3 to continue playing when all other tables have finished playing.

Diversity Cards

Table #3

1. This is a no talking game!
2. Each player gets an equal number of cards. Discard the extra cards. Place your cards in a pile face-down in front of you. When the facilitator says go, turn over the top card to be played with the group (like the card game Spades).
3. Clubs trump all other cards.
4. If a person plays a club, it wins. If two or more people play clubs, the lowest club wins.
5. The lowest card wins.
6. The best card in the deck is the 2 of Hearts.
7. If no Heart is played, the lowest card played wins.
8. If there is a tie – the tied players play again to determine the winner.
9. At the end of the rounds the participant that collects the most number of cards wins the game at this table.
10. When there is a winner, he/she must move to Table #4 to continue playing when all other tables have finished playing.

Diversity Cards

Table #4

1. This is a no talking game!
2. Each player gets an equal number of cards. Discard the extra cards. Place your cards in a pile face-down in front of you. When the facilitator says go, turn over the top card to be played with the group (like the card game Spades).
3. Diamonds trump all other cards.
4. If a person plays a diamond, it wins. If two or more people play diamonds, the lowest diamond wins.
5. The lowest card wins.
6. The best card in the deck is the 2 of Diamonds.
7. If no Diamond is played, the lowest card played wins.
8. If there is a tie – the tied players play again to determine the winner.
9. The participant that collects the most number of cards wins the game at this table.
10. When there is a winner, he/she must move to Table #1 to continue playing when all other tables have finished playing.

Draw Yourself

Participants draw a picture of themselves achieving their greatest goal so that the group can learn more about each other.

Number of Participants: 3-50
Time: 10-15 minutes
Activity Level: Low
Pool Party: Warm the Ice
Props: Colorful Paper, Markers, and Tape

Set Up:
Set the paper and markers in stations around the room so the participants can pick and choose their materials.

Objective:
To draw a picture of yourself achieving your greatest dream.

Step by Step:
1. Ask the participants to draw a picture of themselves achieving their biggest goal or dream.
2. They can be as creative or abstract as they would like to be, and encourage them to be unique.
3. After the group has finished drawing themselves, the group can either take turns explaining their portrait, or the pieces of art can be places in a gallery (usually taped to the wall or hung from a clothesline).
4. When everyone is finished, invite them to participate in a Gallery Walk (pg. 53) to introduce their artwork to the group.

"I learned the value of hard work by working hard." M. Fitzpatrick

Draw Yourself

Questions for Discussion:

- Did you learn something about someone? Who had the dream most similar to yours?

- Do you think this dream or goal will change soon? Why?

- Is it important to share your goals with others? Is it better to keep your goals to yourself?

Facilitator Notes

If using a gallery, implement a gallery walk and act as if the group is at a museum viewing word famous works of art.

Pool Party Variations:

1. **Warm the Ice:** If you would like to be more specific or frame this activity, you can ask them to draw themselves achieving their goals, or at their dream vacation destination, etc.

TRiO Specific Variations:

1. **SSS, EOC, VUB** - Draw yourself is often considered an activity you facilitate with younger groups. Although it certainly works with younger ETS and UB students, it can be easily modified to work with adults. Grab some old magazines and encourage the participants to create a dream board - or a vision board - something that the participant can use to keep track of their dreams and ambitions.

"When the student is ready the teacher will appear." - Zen Proverb

Dream Catcher

This activity is meant to help your participants discover and develop their dreams and goals. Dream Catcher is based on the SMART goals theory that goals and dreams must be Specific, Measurable, Attainable, Relevant, and Time-Bound. (pg. 84)

Number of Participants: Any size
Time: 15-45 minutes (depending how in depth you would like to go with your group.)
Activity Level: Moderate
Pool Party: Warm the Ice
Props: A bucket to act as the Dream Catcher, a throwable for each participant to act as their dream.

Set Up:
Organize participants into a circle and place the bucket in the middle of the circle.

Objective:
For every member of the team to toss their dream (the throwable) in the dream catcher (the bucket) as quickly as possible

Step by Step:
1. While the participants are in the circle, encourage them to think of their dream.
2. During each round the participants are trying to complete the round as quickly as possible and help each participant "achieve" their dream by placing it in the Dream Catcher. This activity will have three timed rounds.

"Happiness is found in doing, not merely possessing." - Unknown

Dream Catcher

Step by Step:

3. **Round 1:** The goal is for each participant to say their dream and place it in the "Dream Catcher."

4. **Round 2:** Challenge the participants to restate their goal, making it more specific and time bound. The team still has the same goal for this round: Each participant says their dream and places it in the "Dream Catcher" as quickly as possible.

5. **Round 3:** This time the group gets even more specific and has the same goal: Each participant says their dream and places it in the "Dream Catcher" as quickly as possible.

Questions for Discussion:

• Were the participants inspired by each other's dreams?

• Were there any ideas or options to help them more quickly "achieve" their dreams?

• Could they have moved the bucket? Are there any things in their actual life that could help them achieve their dreams?

Facilitator Notes:

Between each round, challenge the participants to really think about their dream and start to "own it" by declaring that they will achieve their dream each time they share it with the group. The group always has the goal of completing the activity as quickly as possible while every participant "achieves" their dream.

"If we don't start, it is certain we can't arrive." - Zig Ziglar

Dream Catcher

Facilitator Notes:

They may start out by tossing their dream into the Dream Catcher or even running to the middle to place their dream in the Dream Catcher. Their are no rules on how their dream gets into the Dream Catcher, and they can even pick it up and pass it around the group.

Pool Party Variations:

1. **Break the Ice** - You can use this activity just as a names activity without the actual initiative involved. Play for fun.
2. **Swim** - Do the activity with five rounds and follow the SMART Goal steps - Specific, Measurable, Attainable, Relevant, Time-Bound.

TRiO Specific Variations:

1. **McNair** - Try this as an activity for graduate school goals. What are your research goals? What are your Ph.D. goals?
2. **SSS** - Be specific with collegiate goals. Create categories. What goals do you have with your collegiate finances? Grades? Extracurricular activities? Community involvement?
3. **ETS** - This is great for young participants to help them understand what is the difference between a dream and a goal. Encourage them to start with dreams and then with goals.
4. **UB & UBMS** - Use this as an activity to introduce summer goals. At the beginning of the summer ask them their goals, at the end try the activity again and see if they achieved their goals.

"Know yourself and you will win all battles." - Sun Tzu.

Fill the Basket

Fill the Basket is a collaborative team-building activity that requires participants to plan ahead to achieve a group goal.

Number of Participants: 7-25
Time: 15-25 minutes
Activity Level: Moderate
Pool Party: Swim
Props: 3 Buckets, 30-40 throwables (yarn balls, Beanie Babies, etc.), and tape/rope/webbing to mark the boundary.

Set Up:

Place the tape/rope/webbing in a straight line about 20' long. Place one bucket 5 feet from the line, another bucket 10 feet from the line, and the third bucket 15 feet from the line. The buckets need to be 5 feet apart, thus creating a staggered line of buckets. Lay all of the throwables along the line on the opposite side of the buckets.

Objective:

To hit the team's goal by scoring as many points as possible during each round.

Step by Step:

1. This game is comprised of four (4) one-minute rounds. Each round has different rules, but before each round the group declares a group goal score. Also, before each round suggest a two-minute planning period.

"Fail your way to the top." -Jeff Olsen

Fill the Basket

Step by Step:

Round 1: Instruct the participants that their goal is to score as many points as possible by tossing the throwables into the buckets. They get different points depending upon the buckets.

1. The participants can not cross the line.
2. Once time is up, the participants cannot toss any more throwables.
3. The team gets different points depending upon the buckets.
    *   5 points for throwables tossed into the closest bucket.
    *   10 points for throwables tossed into the middle bucket.
    *   15 points for throwables tossed into the furthest bucket.
4. The participants cannot retrieve any throwables from across the line.
5. If the group throws all items before a minute, the round is over.
6. At the end of the round, encourage the group to help you add up the score. See if their score matches or exceeds their goal score.

Round 2: Follow the rules for Round 1, but challenge the group to reevaluate their approach to the activity and see if they need to make any changes. Ask them to give you a new goal score for Round 2.

1. When the minute is over, ask them if they set an appropriate goal.

"Joy is not in things; it is in us." -Richard Wagner

Fill the Basket

Step by Step:

Round 3: Follow the rules for Round 1, but this time give the team a new resource. Invite three participants to become "runners," teammates who can cross the line and retrieve throwables that have not landed in the bucket.

1. Runners can only retrieve one throwable at a time, and must hand the throwable across the line, not toss it.
2. Encourage the team to pre-plan and then ask for a new group goal score.
3. After the round, ask the group to evaluate their progress and determine the validity of their group goal score.

Round 4: Follow the rules for Round 3 (including the runners), but this time give the group another resource, "Backboards." Three participants will serve as backboards that will straddle the buckets, sitting on their knees with their back to the bucket.

1. Ask for a goal score, and complete the activity.
2. After they are finished, process the activity with a creative and insightful debrief.

Questions for Discussion:

• What was one word to describe Round 1? What about Round 4?

• How did the group communicate during the activity?

"Prejudice is the child of ignorance." -Samuel Hoffenstein

Fill the Basket

Questions for Discussion:

- Did the group allocate adequate time for pre-planning the activity? What pre-planning steps did the group take?

- What ideas did the group find to be the most successful to complete the activity? Which participants developed the ideas?

- How did the new resources change your plan? What action steps did you take to implement the new resources?

- Did any members of the group take charge? Who? How?

Facilitator Notes:

It helps to record the group's scores after each round on a white board or flip chart. This allows the team to see the progress over the rounds.

Some groups need instruction on how to communicate during the planning period. Either provide that instruction or build up to that point throughout the day's activities.

Pool Party Variations:

1. **Break the Ice:** Who doesn't like throwing things into buckets? Try this as just a fun game to get people moving and active.

"It takes a thorn to remove a thorn. -Hindu Proverb

Financial Aid Matching

Financial Aid Matching is an interactive and fun team activity that helps students understand FA terms and acronyms.

Number of Participants: 7-25
Time: 15-25 minutes
Activity Level: Low
Pool Party: Swim
Props: A rope, tape or line to use a starting line, and a set of matching terms (12-15 words over any topic you desire...make sure you have two for each term to complete the match). Make the terms on pieces of colored paper. You can make the terms any size, but we have found it is best to put two words on an 8 1/2 x 11 page, and then cut that page in half so each term has its own page. Make sure the participants cannot see the words through the paper when placed on the floor. See the list below to view sample terms.You can download printable Financial Aid Matching templates at www.myparadigmshift.org/financialaidmatching.

Set Up:

Place the matching terms in a grid on the floor (make sure to have the terms face down so participants can't see the words). Place the rope, tape or line 10-15 feet from the terms parallel to the grid.

Objective:

To match all of the words with your team or entire group.

"Efficiency is intelligent laziness." -David Dunham

Financial Aid Matching

Step by Step:

1. Ask the group to gather behind the rope, tape, or line, and tell them the rules.
2. Only one team member may cross the line at a time.
3. The participant crossing the line turns over two cards, and if the terms match, the group gets to leave the terms face-up. If the terms do not match, they must turn the cards back over facing the floor.
4. The team must uncover all the words to finish the activity.
5. This is a timed activity, and the group must uncover the terms as fast as possible!
6. Encourage your participants to preplan and create systems to become a more efficient team.
7. When finished, I often give the participants a worksheet with definitions of the financial aid terms.

Questions for Discussion:

- What terms have you learned today and what is important as a student?

Pool Party Variations:

1. **Swim:** As the facilitator, you can use whatever terms you would like on the cards. Make this a leadership activity by using terms that describe character, such as integrity, positivity, etc. Do the same to make this activity focus on communication terms, college admission terms, or financial literacy terms.

"Reason and judgment are the qualities of a leader." - Tacitus

Financial Aid Terms:

FAFSA
SEOG
Work Study
Pell Grants
EFC
SAR
Subsidized Loan
Unsubsidized loan
Stafford Loan
Perkins Loan
PLUS Loan
529 College Savings Plan
TEACH Grant
Tribal Grants
Scholarships
Cost of Attendance
Lender
Loan Forgiveness
Financial Need
Prepaid Tuition Plan
Professional Judgment
Student Contribution
Private Loans
Student Loan Debt
Debt Collector

Gallery Walk

Gallery Walks are a great way to create a small gallery around the room so the group can share ideas after an activity or before an event.

Number of Participants: 5-25
Time: 5-10 minutes
Activity Level: Low
Pool Party: Warm the Water
Props: Flip Charts, Tape, Writing Utensils Post-It Notes.

Set Up:
Tape 4 or 5 flip charts on the wall in different places of the room. Place questions at the top of the charts.

Objective:
For the group to review the galleries around the room.

Step by Step:
1. A gallery is a collection of paper, Post-Its, notes, and many other pieces of participant's work taped to the wall or hung from a clothesline.
2. Write different questions on the top of the charts to engage the participants before a workshop.
3. If using a gallery, implement a gallery walk and act as if the group is at a museum viewing word famous works of art.

Pool Party Variations:
1. **Towel Off:** Place questions at the top of the chart to process the group after the end of an activity.

"It's fun being a kid." - Bradford Arthur Angier

Gridwalk

Sometimes our greatest lessons are learned when we make a mistake and keep going forward. Gridwalk teaches our students how to keep going even if they face adversity.

Number of Participants: 5-25
Time: 15-30 minutes
Activity Level: Low-Moderate
Pool Party: Swim
Props: Gridwalk Tarp and Gridwalk Map

Setup:

Purchase a tarp (preferably), a sheet, or just some tape on the ground and make a 7x7 grid of squares with each square being 1 square foot.

Objective:

The goal for the group is to cross the grid as quickly as possible by following the path on the Gridwalk map.

Step by Step:

1. Instruct the participants that the entire group is on a journey. This journey is for everyone to cross the predetermined path on the grid.
2. One participant can step on the grid at a time and participants rotate turns.
3. If a participant steps on the correct square along the path, they can continue their journey.
4. If the participant steps on a wrong square the group starts over from the beginning of the path.

"Beauty is also to be found in a day's work." - Mamie Sypert Burns

Gridwalk

Step by Step:

5. After stepping on a wrong square, the participant leaves the grid in the exact order in which they entered the grid (basically walking the path backwards).

6. If a person does not follow the path correctly on the way off the tarp, they lose their verbal communication for the rest of the activity.

7. After a participant crosses the entire path on the grid and gets to the other side, they lose verbal and nonverbal communication abilities. We do this so that those students who do not pay any attention must pay the consequences.

Questions for Discussion:

• Did you ever step on the wrong square multiple times?

• Are their ever times in your life you feel like you are messing up all of the time?

• How have you learned from your mistakes and changed you behavior?

Facilitator Notes:

When I am designing the Gridwalk path (see below), I try to make sure the participants do not have to repeat steps or go backwards. I like to emphasize the fact that you want to fail forward by moving in a positive direction.

"In great attempts it is glorious even to fail." - Cassius Longinus

Gridwalk

Gridwalk Map
(Feel free to make your own path)

Head, Heart, Hands

We are sometimes guided by our head, sometimes guided by our heart, and sometime our hands. We use this activity as a check-in for the group to see which part of our body has been impacted.

Number of Participants: 2-100
Time: 5 - 15 minutes
Activity Level: Low
Pool Party: Towel Off
Props: None

Objective:

To share with a partner whether you were impacted during the previous activity/day in your head, heart, or hands.

Step by Step:

1. Before, during, or after an activity, ask the participants if they were influenced most in their head (thinking critically), their heart (emotionally), or hands (they are ready for action!).

2. When they decide which area they were influenced, ask them to share with a partner.

Questions for Discussion:

- Is it more important to lead with your head, your heart, or your hands?

- What do you need to use more as a student, your head, heart, or hands?

"Persistent work triumphs. -Virgil

Hey You!

Names are important, but sometimes it is hard to remember everyone in a large group. This is a non-threatening way to learn names.

Number of Participants: 10-30
Time: 5 minutes
Activity Level: Low-Moderate
Pool Party: Break the Ice
Props: None

Set Up:
Ask the participants to circle up and place their right hand in the air.

Objective:
To introduce every person in the group.

Step by Step:
1. One member of the group starts by yelling their name and pointing at someone across the circle who has their hand raised.
2. They run to that person and yell, "Hey You!"
3. That person meets the person pointing at them and gives them a high five while yelling their name.
4. Then they find someone who still has a hand raised and repeats this process. Continue until everyone has been given a high five.

Pool Party Variation:
1. **Swim:** Make this an initiative by making it timed. See how quickly everyone can high five all hands.

"If you choose not to decide, you still made a choice." - N Peart

Human Mastermind

Decision making is a vital part of a successful collegiate career. This activity challenges groups to plan together to achieve a common goal.

Number of Participants: 10-20
Time: 10-15 minutes
Activity Level: Low
Pool Party: Swim
Props: Paper, Writing Utensils

Set Up:
Place four pieces of paper on the floor, and write 1, 2, 3, or 4 on the pages. Before the group starts the activity, pick a person who will stand on each piece of paper (do not share this with the group). Write this down to help you facilitate the activity.

Objective:
To correctly place people on their specific number.

Step by Step:
1. Once the group is ready, tell them that each of them serves a purpose in their quest to achieve this activity. You have selected four people who have the opportunity to represent the group on the different pieces of paper.
2. Ask the group to place one person on each piece of paper, and you will tell them two different things: 1.) How many of them should be on the pages. 2.) How many of them are in the correct position.

"Today, you have 100% of your life left." - Tom Hopkins

Human Mastermind

Step by Step:

3. The group has to get the exact person on each number that you picked earlier.
4. Each time they put four people on the numbers, you tell them the two things.
5. Continue until they get it correct.

Questions for Discussion:

• Did you come up with a plan to solve the problem? What was that plan?

• How important is planning for the decision making process?

• How did you have to work with others to make decisions?

• What things help you make great decisions?

Facilitator Notes:

It is important that the participants know that there is a specific person for each number. Usually groups need a couple of practice rounds to complete understand the activity.

Pool Party Variations:

1. **Swim:** Make Human Mastermind more challenging by timing the activity and counting how many times the group stands on the numbers. This changes the difficulty of the activity, but also the focus. Make sure to process accordingly.

"A candle loses nothing by lighting another candle." - James Keller

Job-oo

Job-oo is based off of the classic board game Taboo. Instead of the group guessing random words like in Taboo, the group will try to guess careers.

Number of Participants: 5-20
Time: 15-25 minutes
Activity Level: Low
Pool Party: Warm the Ice
Props: Timer, Buzzer, Job-oo Cards (You can find all 100 Job-oo Cards at www.myparadigmshift.org/joboo.)

Set Up:

Divide the group into teams alternating around a circle. Pick one player to start as a "Giver."

Objective:

For your team to guess the most careers before time runs out.

Step by Step:

1. Players take turns as the "giver," who attempts to prompt his or her teammates to guess as many careers as possible in the allotted time. However, each card also has "taboo" (forbidden) words listed which may not be spoken.

2. Should the giver say one, a "censor" on the opposing team hits the buzzer and the giver must move on to the next word. For example, the giver might have to get his or her team to deduce the word "attorney" without offering the words "lawyer," "court," or "judge" itself as clues.

"Great minds have purposes, others have wishes." -W. Irving

Job-oo

Step by Step:

3. The giver may only use speech to prompt his or her teammates; gestures, sounds (e.g. barking), or drawings are not allowed. The giver's hints may not rhyme or be an abbreviation with the taboo word.

4. Once the team correctly guesses the word exactly as written on the card, the giver moves on to the next word, trying to get as many words as possible in the allotted time (90 seconds).

5. When time runs out, play passes to the next adjacent player of the other team. The playing team receives one point for correct guesses and one penalty point if "taboo" words are spoken.

Questions for Discussion:

• How did you find ways to describe the jobs?

• How would you describe your dream career?

Facilitator Notes:

You can find some sample Job-oo Cards on the next page, but you can find over 100 printable Job-oo Cards at www.myparadigmshift.org/joboo.

TRiO Specific Variations:

1. **ETS, UB, UBMS** - Create your own Job-oo cards, but this time put a university as the keyword, and descriptive words of the university as "taboo" words. For example, the keyword could be "University of Oklahoma," and the taboo words could be "Sooners," "Norman," or "Football."

"Personal power is the ability to take action." - Anthony Robbins

Job-oo

Attorney

Lawyer
Judge
Courtroom
Jurors
Solicitors

Senator

Government
Congress
Washington DC
Laws
Bills

Nurse

Hospital
Doctor
Patient
Help
Medicine

Dentist

Teeth
Doctor
Cavity
Chair
Clean

Painter

Ladder
Brush
Colors
Bucket
Canvas

Engineer

Create
Fix
Machine
Build
Bridges

Archaeologist

Bones
Dinosaur
Dig
Old
Dirt

Oncologist

Cancer
Doctor
Chemotherapy
Radiation
Hair

Accountant

Tax
Audit
IRS
Finances
CPA

Teacher

Teach
Student
School
Homework
Class

Astronaut

Space
Moon
Rocket
Shuttle
Helmet

Welder

Hot
Metal
Weld
Fuse
Mold

Landmarks

Saint Augustine said, "The world is a book, and those who do not travel read only a page." This engaging and high-energy activity helps groups start to think about a world bigger than themselves.

Number of participants: 9-150
Time: 5-10 minutes
Activity Level: High
Pool Party: Break the Ice
Props: None

Set up:
Divide the group into clusters of 3 participants each. If there are not enough students to make groups of 3, a few groups of 4 will work.

Step by step:
1. After dividing the room into groups, explain that everyone in the room has just become a world-class architect.
2. It is now their task to recreate the world's most impressive landmarks by using only their bodies.
3. To make the game more competitive, tell the participants that it will be a race amongst the groups.
4. Now that the stage is set, call out various landmarks and watch as the participants come up with creative ways to form the called word.
5. Play several rounds and declare winners after each landmark.
6. After a few rounds, rearrange groups and try again.

"Before you do something you must first be something." - Goethe

Landmarks

Step by Step:

7. Some landmarks that we find both engaging and hilarious are on the following :

- Eiffel Tower
- The Pyramids
- The Statue of Liberty
- Stonehenge
- Easter Island Heads
- Sydney Opera House
- Niagara Falls
- The Colosseum

Questions for Discussion:

- How were your designs different from everyone else's?

- How did your team all come up with the same design?

- Is it more important to hold on to your personal idea of what something should look like, or work with a team even if your design might not get picked?

Facilitator Notes:

Take time during the game to show off a few landmarks that were done well. If you don't understand part of a group's landmark, have them share with the other groups.

TRiO Specific Variations:

1. **UBMS** - Landmarks is a great way to introduce the concept of collaborative design to students in a UBMS program. Give each group a piece of paper and a pen, pencil, or marker to draw up the "blueprints" of where each person should be.

"When the flower blooms, the bees come uninvited." - R Krishna

Leader vs. Leader

Leader vs. Leader is a great way to challenge your participants to think about their own leadership abilities by judging the abilities of the greatest leaders of all-time.

Number of Participants: 6-40
Time: 30-40 minutes
Activity Level: Low
Pool Party: Swim
Props: Paper, Writing Utensils

Set Up:
Ask your group to brainstorm a list of the world's greatest all-time leaders. Try to come up with at least as many leaders as you have participants. Place the leaders into a tournament bracket.

Objective:
To determine which leader is the greatest leader of all-time.

Step by Step:
1. After the leaders have been placed into a tournament bracket, encourage the group to decide (through civil conversations) on which leader should advance into the next round.
2. Complete the entire bracket until you have decided the greatest leader of all time.

Questions for Discussion:
• Did you learn anything about a leader? Which one?

"A person who aims at nothing is sure to hit it." - Unknown

Leader vs. Leader

Questions for Discussion:
- Which leader has traits you admire?

- How can you learn from these leaders?

- What is the best way to grow in your leadership skills?

Facilitator Notes:
We have seen this activity go in both directions - participants have engaged in heated discussion…and they have sat in silence.

Often, we will give the group time to research and discuss the leaders before the tournament. This allows the group to have a better opportunity to engage in the conversation about leadership.

Pool Party Variations:
1. **Swim** - Allow the participants to pick a leader with which they resonate. Ask the participants to find a partner. The pair will decide which leader is the greater leader. The group of two then pairs with another set of partners. The four discuss who is the greatest leader. Continue until the group picks one leader as the greatest.

TRiO Specific Variations:
1. **ETS, UB, UBMS** - Try this with different colleges and universities.
2. **SSS. EOC, VUB, McNair** - Try this with different careers within an industry.

"A colt is worth little if it does not break its halter." - Proverb

Likert Scale

There are times before, during, or after an activity when the facilitator needs to check in with the group and Likert Scale fulfills that need.

Number of Participants: 1-100
Time: 1 - 15 minutes
Activity Level: Low
Pool Party: Towel Off
Props: None

Objective:
To rate a participant or group's energy level, engagement, etc., using their own personalized Likert Scale.

Step by Step:
1. Before, during, or after an activity, ask the participants to pull out their Likert Scale.
2. A Likert Scale is made by holding five fingers in the air on both hands. The participants will hold out a number of fingers rating anything the facilitator or group wants to rate.
3. Typically 10 is high and 1 is low, but feel free to mix it up from time to time to measure the participants' focus.

Questions for Discussion:
- On a scale of 1-10, how safe did we play? How was lunch? How was your attitude? How did others communicate with you? How tired are you?

"Doubt is the father of invention." - Galileo

Make a Shake

Make a Shake helps your group learn more about each other and allows the group to cultivate their creativity.

Number of Participants: 2-50
Time: 10- 15 minutes
Activity Level: Low-Moderate
Pool Party: Break the Ice
Props: None

Objective:
To create a secret handshake between two participants.

Step by Step:
1. Have everyone in the group choose a partner (I like to encourage them to partner with someone with a similar sized hand…just for the fun).
2. Ask them to create their own handshake to share with the group.
3. Encourage the participants to be as creative as possible and practice their handshake several times.
4. Go around the circle sharing each person's name and their handshakes.

Pool Party Variations:
1. **Warm the Water** - After partners have finished, have groups of 3 or 4 create small group handshakes. Continue until the entire group has create a handshake.
2. **Towel Off** - Have partners create a handshake that represents their role after an activity.

"Give me the gift of a listening heart." - King Solomon

Name Etymology

What's in a name? This activity dives into the meaning behind our names and how our names define our lives.

Number of Participants: 5-15
Time: 5 - 10 minutes
Activity Level: Low
Pool Party: Warm the Ice
Props: Sheets of paper and writing utensils, and book with definitions of names (optional)

Set Up:

Ask the group to write down their name and then write a paragraph or short story about the history of their name (name origin, who they were named after, unusual nicknames, etc).

Objective:

To find out the meaning of our first, middle, and last names.

Step by Step:

1. When the group is finished researching their names, ask them to share with the group (either as pairs or in large groups).

Questions for Discussion:

• Did you learn anything about your name? What do our names have to do with our story? How can you learn from your family history?

"Share our similarities, celebrate our differences." - M. Scott Peck

One Word Whip

One Word Whip is a very quick way to process a group before, during, or after an activity.

Number of Participants: 5-35
Time: 1 - 3 minutes
Activity Level: Low
Pool Party: Towel Off
Props: None

Set Up:
One Word Whip works best if the group is in a circle.

Objective:
To share your thoughts on a subject using one word.

Step by Step:
1. Standing in a circle, the participants will share their experiences or thoughts using only one word.
2. One participant shares, then the person on their left shares, and then the left again until the entire circle has shared, like a whip around the circle.

Pool Party Variations:
1. **Break the Ice and Warm the Ice** - This activity is great as a processing tool before, during or after an initiative. Or even as a name game. For example, we might ask a group to describe themselves using one word. Or share their middle names. Or what they had for lunch. The idea is to share in a short, concise, and non-threatening way.

"Discipline is remembering what you want." - David Campbell

Paint Swatches

This is a colorful way to discover and process emotions as a group.

Number of Participants: 3-50
Time: 5-10 minutes
Activity Level: Low
Pool Party: Towel Off
Props: Paint Swatches (Lowe's, Home Depot, or Wal-Mart will usually donate these to your collection)

Set Up:
Spread the different paint swatches around the room.

Objective:
For the group to "check in" using the paint swatches.

Step by Step:
1. Encourage the participants to pick a paint swatch that best describes their mood before, during, or after an activity.
2. They can choose one by color or by the name of the color. Encourage the participants to share with the group why they chose their color.

Questions for Discussion:
• Which color best fits your personality?

• Look at the names of the colors. Which one describes how you feel about going to college?

• How does this color explain how you feel right now?

"History will be kind to me for I intend to write it." - W. Churchill

Pit

This wonderful game is based off of the classic card game Pit. Pit emulates the trading floor on the New York Stock Exchange, and is ridiculously fun and full of energy.

Number of Participants: 5-10
Time: 10-15 minutes
Activity Level: High
Pool Party: Break the Ice
Props: Play Money

Set Up:
Give each participant nine bills of the same denomination ($1, $5, $10, $100, etc.)

Objective:
To "corner" the market and collect nine of the same bills.

Step by Step:
1. Shuffle the bills and deal nine to each participant.
2. Open the market by ringing the market bell, or just yelling, "Market is Open!"
3. Start trading cards.
4. A participant can only trade cards by holding out 1, 2, 3, or 4 bills of the same denomination face down.
5. While holding out the bills, the participants will yell the number of bills they are trying to trade (not the denominations in their hand).

"Life is largely a matter of expectation." - Horace

Step by Step:

6. They will then trade bills with someone else who is trying to trade the same number of bills.
7. Once the player has collected all nine of the same bills, they yell "Pit," and the game is stopped.
8. Collect cards, shuffle, and play again.

Facilitator Note:

This game is fast and fun. Sometimes a player can win after only a couple minutes. If this happens, just reshuffle and play again.

Use this game as an introductory activity for a money management lesson. It is perfect to use as a "Break the Ice" activity before you "Swim" in financial literacy or budgeting.

Pool Party Variation:

1. **Warm the Ice** - Give each participant nine index cards and ask them to write their name on the cards. Play the game again, but this time encourage the group to find the nine cards with their name.

TRiO Specific Variation:

1. **ETS, UB, UBMS, SSS** - Try this activity again, but give each participant nine index cards and ask them to write their top strength on all nine cards. Encourage the group to find their strengths. If the group has several players with common strengths, ask them to write their name on the cards as well.

"Everything can be improved." - C. W. Barron

Pitfall

Pitfall explains how avoiding emergencies and wasteful opportunities can lead to building resources - especially money.

Number of Participants: 8-30
Time: 20 - 25 minutes
Activity Level: Low - Moderate
Pool Party: Swim
Props: Tarp with holes cut in it, 15-20 Tennis Balls, Bucket

Set Up:
Set the tarp on the ground about 15-20 feet from the bucket.

Objective:
To transport the tennis balls to the bucket via the tarp.

Step by Step:
1. Instruct the group that they will have the goal of transporting as many dollars (tennis balls) as possible into the bank (bucket) via the tarp (their jobs).
2. The participants must keep ahold of the tarp with both hands throughout the activity.
3. If a tennis ball falls through a hole (ways they lose money in real life), and not into the bucket, the group must start over from behind the start line.
4. A group can not move to the next round unless all tennis balls from the current round are placed into the bucket at the same time.

"Haste in every business brings failure." - Herodotus

Step by Step:

5. The group has 15 minutes to complete this activity.
6. The group has a mandatory 2-minute planning period before the 15-minute timed period starts.
7. The tennis balls must start from the corner of the tarp.
8. The group picks up the tarp, holding only the edges as the facilitator places one tennis ball on any corner of the tarp.
9. The group must then transport the tennis ball to the bucket via the tarp.
10. If the team can drop the tennis ball into the bucket before it falls through to the floor the team will get one point.
11. After each successful round, the facilitator will increase the number of tennis balls on the tarp, thus increasing the team's chances of scoring points.

Questions for Discussion:

• What areas in your life do find yourself consistently losing money?

• How do you avoid pitfalls with your money?

• How do you work with others to save your money?

• Did you try to get greedy during the activity? What areas of your life might you be greedy?

• How important is money in your life?

"Happiness is not a goal, it is a by-product." - Eleanor Roosevelt

Pitfall

Facilitator Notes:

It is great to use the money analogy throughout the entire activity. If they lose a tennis ball, they are losing money. The holes in the tarp are ways they lose money when not working. The bucket is the bank.

Pool Party Variations:

1. **Swim** - Try this as an activity without the emphasis on money, but with an emphasis on goal setting. After hearing the rules, how many tennis balls do they think they could drop into the bucket?

2. **Swim** - Make Pitfall a competition between two groups. Afterwards, process the emotions they felt while competing. How do you handle pressure and competition?

3. **Swim** - Place 15 tennis balls on the tarp and see how long the group can keep them on the tarp without dropping through a hole.

4. **Towel Off** - After an activity, place a tennis ball on the tarp. One of the individuals can share their thoughts for as long as a tennis ball remains on the tarp. Once the ball falls through a hole, place another on the tarp and another player can share.

TRiO Specific Variations:

1. **ETS, UB, UBMS** - Try this activity with a college-going twist. Their goal is to accomplish the things they need to do to attend college (apply, take ACT/SAT, FAFSA, etc.) Each item they need to accomplish is a tennis ball and the group has to get all of them into the bucket.

"Anything one can imagine, other's can make real." - J. Verne

Plan That Mine

Planning is an important part of the college-going process. This activity expresses how to use your resources to accomplish the steps necessary to succeed.

Number of Participants: 5-30
Time: 15-30 minutes
Activity Level: Moderate
Pool Party: Swim
Props: Paper Plates, Throwables, Writing Utensils, Blindfolds, & Tape, Rope or Webbing for Barriers

Set Up:

Two ropes as parallel barriers set up about 15-20 feet apart. Eventually scatter the paper plates and throwables randomly between the barriers.

Objective:

To get the entire team from their start position across the mines as quickly as possible while planning their best direct route.

Step by Step:

1. Before starting the activity, label one set of objects as items that must be accomplished, called "goals", in a certain order (take ACT, complete FAFSA, etc.)
2. Label another set of objects as distractions (recreation, procrastination, etc.). Feel free to let students offer suggestions for these.
3. Distribute the "mines" and "distractions" between the two ropes.

"Dream as if you'll live forever, live as if you'll die today." - J. Dean

Plan That Mine

Step by Step:

4. Students work as one team, pairs, or two teams to accomplish the task below.
5. The team tries to gather all of the "goals" in the proper order, and deliver them to the other side.
6. A team member can only cross the barrier blindfolded.
7. One participant is guiding another through the minefield using verbal cues.
8. If a participant steps on a mine, they start over.
9. If they select the correct goal, they deliver the goal to the opposite side.
10. Only goals used for planning purposes can be moved, distraction mines cannot.
11. The next student is blindfolded and continues in relay race style.

Questions for Discussion:

- What are the steps needed to go to college?

- How can you work with others to accomplish your goal of getting to college?

- Is it hard for you to trust others?

Facilitator Note:

****A trust activity like Plan That Mine should not be facilitated until the group has built a level of trust. Allow the participants to have the choice to wear a blindfold. If a participant feels unsafe, encourage them to stop and open their eyes.

"You can accomplish by kindness what you can't by force." - Syrus

Plumber Pete

Name games are a vital part of any program. Plumber Pete combines a name game with an opportunity to talk about careers. It is a perfect combination.

Number of Participants: 5-25
Time: 15-30 minutes
Activity Level: Moderate
Pool Party: Break the Ice
Props: None

Set Up:
Ask the group to get into a circle (or square if that suits you best).

Objective:
To introduce yourself to the group with a career and a motion that matches your name.

Step by Step:
1. Encourage each participant to think of a career that starts with the same first letter as their first name.
2. If you are Plumber Pete you will introduce yourself to the group and make a motion that would show the group you are in fact a plumber (i.e. plunging a toilet, fixing a sink, etc.).
3. After the participant introduces their name and new career, the group must say hello to "Plumber Pete" and mimic their motion. Encourage the participants to be as creative as possible, and try to find new careers.

"Every chance taken is another chance to win." - Unknown

Popcorn

Popcorn is a must-have initiative for facilitators of all skill levels and is a fun, interactive activity for groups of all sizes. Popcorn expresses how life changes from your first year to your last year in school.

Number of Participants: 5-20
Time: 20-30 minutes
Activity Level: High
Pool Party: Swim
Props: Bucket, Small Rope (15-20'), Enough small Wiffle and large Wiffle balls to fill the bucket.

Set Up:

Place a bucket in the middle of an open area on the floor. Place a rope circle around the bucket that is about 5-7 feet in diameter. The bucket will be almost overflowing with Wiffle balls.

Objective:

As a group, participants will bounce the Wiffle balls inside the rope circle and into the bucket as quickly as possible during four rounds.

Step by Step:

1. There are four one-minute rounds.
2. Before the timed round starts, the facilitator will empty the bucket all over the room.
3. As soon as the bucket is emptied, the one-minute timer begins.

"Fate leads the willing, and drags along the reluctant." - Seneca

Popcorn

Step by Step:

4. During each round the participants try to refill the bucket by bouncing the Wiffle balls into the rope circle and then into the bucket (shooting without bounding is prohibited).

5. The participants stand outside the rope circle and the bucket and rope cannot move.

6. If a participant is holding a Wiffle ball, they can not move their feet. They are stuck in that position until they get rid of the ball.

7. When each one-minute round is over, the group must stop throwing the Wiffle balls.

8. Continue for four rounds, and track the progress of each round.

Questions for Discussion:

• What word best describes round 1?

• What word best describes round 4?

• How does this compare to your first year of college? What about your fourth year?

• What actions or plans did you implement to become more efficient and productive?

• What could have been done to improve the team's performance?

• If you were teaching a new team how to complete this activity, what things would you tell the team?

"Don't believe in miracles - depend on them." - Laurence J. Peter

Popcorn

Facilitator Notes:

I encourage the team to take time before each round to plan for the upcoming round. This will allow for the participants to share ideas, devise plans, and develop techniques to quickly complete the round.

The best way for the team to complete this activity is if the participants lay around the bucket, creating a barrier that keeps the balls from scattering across the room.

I typically compare round one to their first year of high school or college. The same words they used to describe the first round: fun, exciting, chaotic, unorganized, new, confusing, crazy, etc.

I parallel the words they used to describe round four to describe their fourth year of high school or college. It will be organized, efficient, successful. Then we discuss the things they can do from their freshman year to their senior year to become more successful.

This activity only works if done on a hard surface. This does not really work effectively on grass or extremely soft carpet.

Pool Party Variation:

1. **Swim:** For very large groups you can use more than one Popcorn kit, and Wiffle balls could go to either bucket. All the other rules apply for the larger groups.

"Weakness of attitude becomes weakness of character." - Einstein

Post an Emotion

Post an Emotion encourages a group to post their emotions so the entire group is aware of how they feel.

Number of Participants: 5-45
Time: 5-10 minutes
Activity Level: Low
Pool Party: Towel Off
Props: Post-It Notes, Writing Utensils

Set Up:
Place Post-It Notes in piles around the room and give each participant a writing utensil.

Objective:
To post your emotions so others can see.

Step by Step:
1. Ask participants to share an emotion by writing one word on a Post-It note.
2. Ask the participants to stick the Post-It note somewhere on their shirt.
3. Ask your group to mingle about the room and shake hands with other people.
4. Encourage your participants to be candid and share with the group why they wrote the different emotions.

TRiO-Specific Variations:
1. **ETS, UB, UBMS** - Some groups are not mature enough to handle this activity. Instead of emotions, ask them to post their strengths.

"Where there are friends, there is wealth." - Titus Muccius Plautus

Post-It Party

Post-It Party is the follow up activity to Post an Emotion (pg. 84). It gives the entire group an opportunity to share together.

Number of Participants: 5-45
Time: 5-10 minutes
Activity Level: Low
Pool Party: Towel Off
Props: Post-It Notes, Writing Utensils

Set Up:
Place Post-It Notes in piles around the room and give each participant a writing utensil.

Objective:
To post your emotions in a gallery (pg. 53) so the entire group can see.

Step by Step:
1. Ask participants to share an emotion by writing one word on a Post-It note.
2. Ask the participants to stick the Post-It note somewhere in the gallery.
3. After completing a different initiative or completing a day, encourage the participants to go to the gallery and find a Post-It that best describes their feelings at that moment. It does not have to be one that they previously posted.
4. Ask your group to mingle about the room and shake hands with other people.

"Where there are friends, there is wealth." - Titus Muccius Plautus

Quadrants

Quadrants is an interactive time-management activity that shows students how to prioritize their time.

Number of Participants: 5-30
Time: 30-45minutes
Activity Level: Low
Pool Party: Swim
Props: Quadrants Worksheet

Set Up:
Place a large Quadrants Activity Chart on the wall or dry-erase board and give each person a blank chart.

Objective:
To determine what is important, not important, urgent and not urgent.

Step by Step:
For those who are not familiar with quadrants, here is a picture and a brief overview.

	Urgent	Not Urgent
Important	Paying Bills Crying Baby Commute to Work Kitchen Fire	Vacation Exercise Organization Planning
Not Important	Interruptions Flat Tire Solicitor Calls Distractions	Video Games Social Media Busy Work Trivia

"The discipline of desire is the background of character." - Locke

Quadrants

Step by Step:

1. Ask the participants to think about and write down the things that occupy their time.

2. Once the list is complete, ask the participants to place their activities in one of the four quadrants.

3. In **Quadrant 1** (top left) we have important, urgent items – items that **need to be dealt with immediately.**

4. In **Quadrant 2** (top right) we have important, but not urgent items – items that are important but do not require your immediate attention, and **need to be planned for**.

5. In **Quadrant 3** (bottom left) we have urgent, but unimportant items -items which **should be minimized or eliminated.** These are the time sucks, the "poor planning on your part does not constitute an emergency on my part" variety of tasks.

6. In **Quadrant 4** (bottom right) we have unimportant and also not urgent items – items that don't have to be done anytime soon, perhaps add little to no value and also **should be minimized or eliminated**.

7. Next, ask the group to write down the items they want to pursue. How do they fit into the quadrants?

Questions for Discussion:

• Which quadrant do you spend most of your time?

• What activities take up most of your time?

"Happiness is not pleasure, it's victory." - Zig Ziglar

Quadrants

Questions for Discussion:

• Which quadrant do you want to spend the majority of your time in?

• What activities should you drop from your list?

• Which activities do you want to spend more time doing?

• How do you add new activities to your life without getting overwhelmed?

Facilitator Notes:

We first learned about Quadrants in Stephen Covey's wonderful book, *The Seven Habits of Highly Effective People*. Obviously, if you read this book you will have a better grasp on this activity.

It is sometimes helpful to provide examples of the activities your participants pursue. Really challenge the group to come up with all of the things they do in an average week.

TRiO Specific Variations:

1. **ETS, UB, UBMS** - Start this activity by asking the participants to fill out a 24-hour chart with their typical daily activities. If necessary, ask them to keep track of their activities for an entire week.

"What you are will show in what you do." - Thomas Alva Edison

Saying Goodbye

Saying Goodbye is a very simple way for your group to anonymously post nice comments about other participants.

Number of Participants: 5 and up
Time: 15-25 minutes
Activity Level: Low
Pool Party: Towel Off
Props: Paper, Markers, Tape

Set Up:
Write each participant's name on a piece of paper, and hang that paper on the wall.

Objective:
To leave positive remarks on another participant's paper that is hanging around the room.

Step by Step:
1. Ask the participants to write their name on a piece of paper and hang it on the wall. If the group has enough time, encourage them to decorate their paper if they desire.
2. Throughout the day, encourage participants to write positive remarks on someone's paper if they noticed something worthy of a kind and genuine comment.
3. At the end of the day, encourage the participants to read their paper and take it home as a keepsake of the day's events.

"No one ever went broke by saying no too often." - Harvey Mckay

Show Me The Money

Show Me The Money uses fake money as an opportunity to set financial goals.

Number of Participants: 2-50
Time: 5-10 minutes
Activity Level: Low
Pool Party: Warm the Water
Props: Fake Money & Writing Utensils

Set Up:
Place a pile of fake money on the floor in the middle of the room.

Objective:
Use fake money to set financial goals.

Step by Step:
1. Spread the play money about the floor.
2. Gather the participants around the money and ask them to grab as many as they feel is necessary.
3. Leave this vague and allow them to decide how much they feel is necessary.
4. Encourage the participants to write a financial goal they have on **each** bill.
5. When finished, encourage the participants to share what they have just processed

Pool Party Variations:
1. **Towel Off** - Use the money as a processing tool after a money-related activity. Encourage the group to write down their thoughts to save for later.

"There's nobody "out there." It's all in here." - Mal Pancoast

SMART Goal Paper Fold

Almost everyone has a goal or a dream, but do not know how to turn them into SMART Goals. This activity will help participants make their goals more specific, measurable, attainable, relevant, and time-bound.

Number of Participants: 1-Unlimited
Time: 15-25 minutes
Activity Level: Low
Pool Party: Swim
Props: A Piece of Paper (any size will work, but the larger the better) & Writing Utensils.

Set Up:
Give each participant paper and pen.

Objective:
Use this interactive activity to help participants make their goals SMART goals. (Specific, Measurable, Attainable, Relevant, Time-Bound)

Step by Step:
1. Give participants a piece of paper and ask them to fold the paper in half four times.
2. Instruct the participants to write their goal on one side of the folded paper. They can write it out, illustrate it, or be as creative as possible. (Example goal: Go to college)
3. Ask the participants to flip the paper over, and write down a goal that is more specific. (Example: Go to Baylor and major in Nursing)

"Finite to fail, but infinite to venture." - Emily Dickinson

SMART Goal Paper Fold

Step by Step:

4. Encourage the participants to unfold the paper once and make their goal measurable on the blank side of the paper. (Example: Go to Baylor, major in nursing, and graduate magna cum laude)

5. Invite the participants to unfold their paper one more time, flip it over, and make sure their goal is attainable by writing down examples of things they know they can do to achieve their goal. (Example: I have graduated HS, I excel in science and math, etc.)

6. Ask the participants to unfold the paper once more, flip it over, and now make sure their goal is relevant. This is the "why" of the SMART Goal. Why would you want to achieve this goal? (Example: Write reasons why they want to accomplish this goal: More money for my family, better career, etc.)

7. Ask them to once again unfold their paper and make their goal time-bound. (Example: Go to Baylor, major in nursing, and graduate magna cum laude by May 1, 2016)

8. Once they have written down their new SMART Goal. Ask them to sign the paper and date it for review in the future.

9. After the activity, the participants should now have a piece of paper with their SMART Goal, some factors that say how they could achieve the goal (attainable), their reasons for attaining that goal (relevant), and a date to accomplish the goal (time-bound).

"Problems are not stop signs, they are guidelines." -Robert Schuller

SMART Goal Paper Fold

Questions for Discussion:

- What did it feel like once you had a SMART Goal?

- Do you feel like you are closer to achieving your goal now?

- What is the next action step now that you have a SMART Goal?

- What were some of the things on your relevant page?

- Why do you want to achieve this goal?

- Who can help you achieve this goal?

Facilitator Notes:

It is usually beneficial to combine this workshop with a brief introduction to SMART Goals. It works to explain SMART Goals either before the activity, or as a step-by-step guide during the initiative.

TRiO Specific Variations:

1. **ETS, UB, UBMS** - Encourage participants to draw or paint their goals, this will help them become more realistic. Bring old magazines and newspapers, scissors, and glue to let the participants make their last page into an art masterpiece.

"Fall seven times; stand up eight. -Japanese Proverb

Snakes

Snakes is a trust activity that focuses on non-verbal communication and how messages can get lost while going from person to person.

Number of Participants: 2-30
Time: 10-15 minutes
Activity Level: Low - Moderate
Pool Party: Swim
Props: Blindfolds, Throwables, Buckets, Rope/Tape for barrier

Set Up:
Create a large circle barrier with the tape or a rope. Place a bucket in the middle of the circle. Toss the throwables randomly inside the barrier.

Objective:
For every member of the team to place a throwable into the bucket.

Step by Step:
1. Depending on the amount of people in the group, ask the participants to get into teams of 5-7 people.
2. Ask the participants to stand in a single file line and place their hands on the shoulders of the person in front of them.
3. All participants will be blindfolded (or eyes shut) except for the person standing in the very back of the line.
4. This is a no-talking activity, but allow the group to take 1-2 minutes to pre-plan.

"I don't eat junk foods and I don't think junk thoughts." - Pilgrims

Snakes

Step by Step:

5. The person in the back of the line will guide the participants around the circle barrier by simply tapping the shoulders of the person in front of them.

6. That person will tap the shoulders of the person in front of them, and so on, until the person in the front of the line will move towards a throwable.

7. When a throwable is approached, the person in the front will grab the throwable and then be guided to the bucket where they will drop the throwable.

8. When a participant drops the throwable into the bucket, they will then remove their blindfold and move to the back of the line and become the sighted team member. The person who was in the back of the line then puts on a blindfold.

9. Continue this process until all team members have placed a throwable into the bucket.

10. If there is more than one team, the first team to finish is the winner and then should encourage the other teams until they are finished.

11. If the teams are uneven, the team with the least amount of members will continue to rotate until they have dropped as many throwables into the bucket as the largest team would have to drop into the bucket.

Questions for Discussion:

• How did your team communicate?

• What did it feel like to not be in control?

"To the timid soul, nothing is possible." - John Bach

Snakes

Questions for Discussion:

- What ways did the group lose communication down the line?

- How do you best communicate with your friends or family?

- Do you know anyone who is a great communicator? What do they do well?

- What does non-verbal communication have to do with communication?

- What ways do we communicate non-verbally?

Facilitator Notes:

*****It is very important to ensure and instill a sense of trust within the group before attempting this activity. Please do not try Snakes before building trust on a smaller/safer level.

TRiO Specific Variations:

1. **SSS, EOC** - You can try this activity without blindfolds and without an open space. Invite the participants to sit in a row, side by side. Give the first person in the line instructions to a task. They will non-verbally pass the instructions down the line. The last person will complete the task as explained by the group.

"Rule your mind or it will rule you." - Horace

Take a Stand

Adding props to a debrief or processing activity can often help participants open up to the rest of the group. Take A Stand debrief utilizes props to create conversations about an activity, initiative, or even at the end of a day.

Number of Participants: 2-50
Time: 5-20 minutes
Activity Level: Low
Pool Party: Towel Off
Props: Any prop that you have handy

Set Up:
Place several throwables or random items around the room.

Objective:
To encourage the group to process an activity

Step by Step:
1. The object of this debrief is to encourage the participants to stand by a throwable or item around the room.
2. Each item will have a specific meaning or description pertaining to the previous activity or sequence of activities.
3. After the participants take a stand by the item, they discuss their thoughts with the others standing by them.
4. This creates an opportunity for participants to process their thoughts with like-minded individuals.

"We must become the change we want to see." - Gandhi

Take a Stand

Facilitator's Notes:

Example: Place a red, green, and yellow throwable in three different areas of the room. Ask the participants to stand by the red throwable if they felt frustrated or if the activity halted their progress, to stand by the yellow if they were confused by the activity, and to stand by the green if they felt like they completely understood and enjoyed the activity.

Be creative with your props and you will be surprised by the participants' in-depth answers. Use photos, numbers, toys, books, etc. as props.

Pool Party Variations:

1. **Warm the Water** - Use this exact same activity, but as a "Get-to-Know-You" activity. Place items around the room and ask questions pertaining to the props. For example: Grab a stapler, a tape dispenser, and an eraser. Ask the participants to stand next to the item that describes their work ethic.

"Only the hand that erases can write the true thing." - M. Eckhart

Talking Toys

Use all of your old toys to help your group process after an activity.

Number of Participants: 5-25
Time: 10-25 minutes
Activity Level: Low
Pool Party: Towel Off
Props: Random Assortment of Toys

Set Up:
Place the toys around the room.

Objective:
To process an activity or workshop with random toys.

Step by Step:
1. After an activity or workshop ask participants to find a toy that best describes their feelings or emotions. Use the toys for any processing opportunity.

Facilitator Notes:
This may seem like a silly or childish activity, but we are often amazed at how quickly groups being to share after seeing the toys of their childhood.

Pool Party Variations:
1. **Warm the Ice** - Use this as a way for groups to get to know each other better. Ask the participants to grab a toy that fits their personality.

"Rest is the sweet sauce of labor. -Plutarch

Tongue in Cheek

The goal for your group during this fun yet challenging name game is for each participant to say their name aloud without saying it at the same time as another participant.

Number of Participants: 5-20
Time: 10-25 minutes
Activity Level: Low
Pool Party: Break the Ice
Props: None

Set Up:
Ask the group to get into a circle.

Objective:
For everyone in the group to say their name without speaking at the same time as someone else.

Step by Step:
1. Ask the participants to say their name out loud.
2. If the group members can each say their name the game is completed, however, if two or more participants say their name at the same time, the group must start over.
3. Make it clear to the group that no order, strategy or plan should be implemented to complete the activity.
4. Ask a participant to start by saying their name, and see if the group can make it all the way through.

"Are you green and growing or ripe and rotting?" - Ray Kroc

Web of Names

Web of Names is an easy group initiative that focuses on learning the names of the people in the group.

Number of Participants: 5-25
Time: 5-10 minutes
Activity Level: Low-Moderate
Pool Party: Break the Ice
Props: Rope

Set Up:
Ask the group to gather in a circle.

Objective:
To get to know the names of other group members, and to untangle the rope.

Step by Step:
1. The facilitator starts out holding a rope and passes it to someone else in the group.
2. This person introduces themselves to the group, holds their part of their rope, and throws the rest to someone else.
3. Continue in this manner until everyone is holding the rope and has introduced themselves to the group.
4. The last person will throw the remaining length of rope to the facilitator.
5. At this point, the group will untangle the rope without letting go of their portion.
6. Use this time to encourage the participants to share interesting facts with other group members.

"Happiness or unhappiness is often a matter of choice."-Unknown

You Get a Prize

This activity utilizes the great materials TRiO gives to its participants. Instead of just handing out backpacks, pens, and notebooks…reward the participants who engage.

Number of Participants: 2-40
Time: 5-10 minutes
Activity Level: Low
Pool Party: Towel Off
Props: Anything you would use as a prize or a prop to link to the next activity.

Set Up:
Place all of the educational products on a table for the participants to observe.

Objective:
To encourage participants to share after an activity.

Step by Step:
1. To encourage someone to talk before or after an activity, the facilitator will hand/toss/throw a "prize" to the participant who shared.

Facilitator Notes:
As a ETS staff member, we found that our students appreciated the materials we would provide, but we wanted a way to reward the participants who were engaged in our program. We created a culture that rewarded students who actively participated.

"A hard beginning maketh a good ending." - John Heywood

Lesson Plans

Every good activity needs a good lesson plan. We have combined the activities in this book into 16 brand-new lesson plans for TRiO Programs.

Each lesson plan follows the Pool Party Process, and will have one activity to Break the Ice (engage the participants), one to Warm the Water (build rapport), one to Swim (learn), and one to Towel Off (process the group).

Each lesson plan is roughly one to two hours worth of activities, and is specific to the needs of all of the TRiO Programs.

The following categories will be included in each Lesson Plan.

Workshop Title:
The title of the workshop used for promotional materials.

Workshop Category:
The lesson plans can be placed under the following categories:
- Life Skills
- College Success
- High School Planning
- Career Planning

Number of Participants:
Number of participants that would be ideal for the workshop.

"There is no time like the pleasant." - Oliver Herford

Lesson Plans

Length of Workshop:
Each workshop will be roughly one to two hours in length.

Space Required:
How much space you will need for the activity. The space will either be a classroom, an open space, or gym.

Props Needed:
The total resources needed to facilitate the activities with your group.

Activities:
The list of activities by Pool Party Process which includes a brief write-up of the activities. Also included will be the page number where you can find the activities. (Note: some activities will be variations of the original activity.)

"Lost time is never found again." - Proverb

Career Connections

Workshop Title:
Career Connections - How To Find the Right Career

Workshop Category: Career Planning
Number of Participants: 10-25
Length of Workshop: 75 minutes
Space Required: Classroom
Props Needed: Timer, Careeragories Worksheet, Writing Utensils, Dry Erase Board or Butcher Paper, Candy

Activities:
Break the Ice: Plumber Pete (pg. 80)
Plumber Pete combines a name game with an opportunity to talk about careers.

Warm the Water: Careeragories (pg. 24)
Careeragories is based off of the popular game Scattergories in which the players try to guess as many jobs that start with the letter chosen. Use this as an opportunity to introduce careers to your group.

Swim: Candy Factory (pg. 22)
Candy Factory is an interactive brainstorming activity that helps participants understand the scale of job opportunities in a particular area.

Towel Off: One Word Whip (pg. 71)
One Word Whip is a very quick way to process a group before, during, or after an activity.

"Every calling is great when greatly pursued. -O. Wendell Holmes

Workshop Title:

College Admissions - What Really Matters When Choosing a College

Workshop Category: College Success
Number of Participants: 5-20
Length of Workshop: 60 minutes
Space Required: Classroom
Props Needed: Random Used Toys, College Admissions Rank 'Em Cards, Fake Money

Activities:

Break the Ice: One Word Whip (pg. 71)
One Word Whip is a very quick way to process a group before, during, or after an activity.

Warm the Water: Talking Toys (pg. 99)
Use all of your old toys to help your group get to know each other before an activity.

Swim: College Admissions Rank 'Em (pg. 27)
College Admissions Rank 'Em will start the conversation amongst students about the different reasons for deciding on a future college.

Towel Off: Show Me The Money (pg. 83)
Use the money as a processing tool after an activity. Encourage the group to write down their thoughts to save for later.

"The pursuit of perfection often impedes improvement." - G. Will

Communication Skills

Workshop Title:
Communication Skills - How to use Verbal and Non-Verbal Communication to as Work as a Group

Workshop Category: Life Skills
Number of Participants: 12-24
Length of Workshop: 75 minutes
Space Required: Open Space
Props Needed: Rope or Webbing, Construction Paper, Markers, Tape

Activities:
Break the Ice: Web of Names (pg. 94)
Web of Names is an easy group initiative that focuses on learning the names of the people in the group.

Warm the Water: Draw Yourself (pg. 41)
Participants draw a picture of themselves achieving their greatest goal so that the group can learn more about each other.

Swim: Human Mastermind (pg. 59)
Decision making is a vital part of a successful collegiate career. This activity challenges groups to plan together to achieve a common goal.

Towel Off: Saying Goodbye (pg. 89)
Saying Goodbye is a very simple way for your group to anonymously post nice comments about other participants.

"Do the thing and you will have the power." - R. Waldo Emerson

Community Learning

Workshop Title:
Community Learning - How to Grow as an Individual to Grow Your Community

Workshop Category: Life Skills
Number of Participants: 15-45
Length of Workshop: 60 minutes
Space Required: Classroom
Props Needed: Jar of Beans, Post-It Notes, Writing Utensils

Activities:
Break the Ice: Landmarks (pg. 64)
This engaging and high-energy activity helps groups start to think about a world bigger than themselves.

Warm the Water: Name Etymology (pg. 70)
What's in a name? This activity dives into the meaning behind our names and how our names define our lives.

Swim: Count the Beans (pg. 30)
Count the Beans shows your group that the collective is greater than the individual. The participants guess how many beans are in a jar and then collaborate with other participants to get the closest guess.

Towel Off: Post an Emotion (pg. 84)
Post an Emotion encourages a group to post their emotions so the entire group is aware of how they feel.

"For every disciplined effort there is a multiple reward."- Jim Rohn

Decision Making

Workshop Title:
Decision Making - Practical Steps to Making Great Decisions

Workshop Category: Life Skills
Number of Participants: 10-25
Length of Workshop: 60 minutes
Space Required: Open Space
Props Needed: Gridwalk Tarp, Butcher Paper, Markers, Post-Its, Writing Utensils

Activities:
Break the Ice: Make a Shake (pg. 69)
Make a Shake helps your group learn more about each other and allows the group to cultivate their creativity.

Warm the Water: Gallery Walk (pg. 53)
Gallery Walks are a great way to create a small gallery around the room so the group can share ideas after an activity or before an event.

Swim: Gridwalk (pg. 54)
Sometimes our greatest lessons are learned when we make a mistake and keep going forward. Gridwalk teaches our students how to keep going even if they face adversity.

Towel Off: Post-It Party (pg. 85)
Post-It Party is the follow up activity to Post an Emotion (pg. 84). It gives the entire group an opportunity to share together.

"I think and that is all that I am. -Wayne Dyer

Diversity Awareness

Workshop Title:

Diversity Awareness - What are the Unwritten Rules of Society and Culture?

Workshop Category: Life Skills
Number of Participants: 16-32
Length of Workshop: 60 minutes
Space Required: Classroom
Props Needed: Bucket, Throwables, Paper Plates, Ropes

Activities:

Break the Ice: Pit (pg. 73)
Use this variation of Pit to Break the Ice. Give the participants nine index cards and ask them to write down one word on all cards that describes their culture.

Warm the Water: One Word Whip (pg. 71)
One Word Whip is a very quick way to process a group before, during, or after an activity.

Swim: Diversity Cards (pg. 34)
This activity is perfect for a facilitator who wants to discuss cultural diversity, written and unwritten rules in society, and social norms within a group.

Towel Off: Talking Toys (pg. 99)
Use all of your old toys to help your group process after an activity.

"Attempt the impossible only to improve your work." - Bette Davis

Financial Aid

Workshop Title:
Financial Aid - How to Understand the Inner-Workings of Grants, Scholarships, and Student Loans

Workshop Category: College Success
Number of Participants: 10-40
Length of Workshop: 60 minutes
Space Required: Open Space
Props Needed: Ropes, Financial Aid Matching Cards, Fake Money, Paint Swatches, Writing Utensils

Activities:
Break the Ice: Tongue in Cheek (pg. 100)
The goal for your group during this fun yet challenging name game is for each participant to say their name aloud without saying it at the same time as another participant.

Warm the Water: Show Me the Money (pg. 90)
Show Me The Money uses fake money as an opportunity to set financial goals.

Swim: Financial Aid Matching (pg. 50)
Financial Aid Matching is an interactive and fun team activity that helps students understand FA terms and acronyms.

Towel Off: Paint Swatches (pg. 72)
This is a colorful way to discover and process emotions as a group.

"It is not the position, but the disposition." - J. E. Dingerl

Goal Setting

Workshop Title:
Goal Setting - How to set Goals to Accelerate Your Future

Workshop Category: Life Skills
Number of Participants: 10-60
Length of Workshop: 60 minutes
Space Required: Gymnasium
Props Needed: Ropes, Financial Aid Matching Cards, Fake Money, Paint Swatches, Writing Utensils

Activities:
Break the Ice: Hey You! (pg. 58)
Names are important, but sometimes it is hard to remember everyone in a large group. This is a non-threatening way to learn names.

Warm the Water: Name Etymology (pg. 70)
What's in a name? This activity dives into the meaning behind our names and how our names define our lives.

Swim: Fill the Basket (pg. 46)
Fill the Basket is a collaborative team-building activity that requires participants to plan ahead to achieve a group goal.

Towel Off: Make a Shake (pg. 69)
Have partners create a handshake that represents their role after an activity.

"Time ripens all things, no man is born wise." - M. de Cervantes

Workshop Title:
High School Success - How to Learn From Others to Graduate

Workshop Category: High School Success
Number of Participants: 5-25
Length of Workshop: 60 minutes
Space Required: Gymnasium
Props Needed: Bucket, Throwables, Plates, Ropes

Activities:
Break the Ice: Plumber Pete (pg. 80)
Use this variation to introduce participants to each other. Instead of using a career-based adjective in front of your name, try one that describes your personality.

Warm the Water: Take a Stand (pg. 97)
Use this exact same activity, but as a "Get-to-Know-You" activity. Place items around the room and ask questions pertaining to the props.

Swim: Popcorn (pg. 81)
Popcorn expresses how life changes from your first year to your last year in school.

Towel Off: Head, Heart, Hands (pg. 57)
We are sometimes guided by our head, sometimes guided by our heart, and sometime our hands. Use this check-in to see which part has been impacted.

"It's never too late to become what you might have been." G. Eliot

Leadership

Workshop Title:
Leadership - How Can You Learn From Leaders of the Past to Improve Our Personal Leadership

Workshop Category: Life Skills
Number of Participants: 10-20
Length of Workshop: 60 minutes
Space Required: Classroom
Props Needed: Paper, Writing Utensils, Butcher Paper, Markers

Activities:
Break the Ice: One Word Whip (pg. 71)
One Word Whip is a very quick way to process a group before, during, or after an activity. Ask the group to use one word that describes leadership.

Warm the Water: Make a Shake (pg. 69)
Ask the group to create a handshake that displays their leadership skills.

Swim: Leader vs. Leader (pg. 66)
Leader vs. Leader is a great way to challenge your participants to think about their own leadership abilities by judging the abilities of the greatest leaders of all-time.

Towel Off: Candy Factory (pg. 22)
Use Candy Factory as a processing tool after another activity. Ask the participants to share the different experiences they observed.

"Confidence is a very fragile thing." - Joe Montana

Managing Money

Workshop Title:
Managing Money - How To Avoid Money Pitfalls to Save Money

Workshop Category: Life Skills
Number of Participants: 15-30
Length of Workshop: 90 minutes
Space Required: Gymnasium
Props Needed: Tarp with Holes, Bucket, Tennis Balls, Fake Money, Giveaways, Writing Utensils

Activities:
Break the Ice: Pit (pg. 73)
This wonderful game is based off of the classic card game Pit. Pit emulates the trading floor on the New York Stock Exchange, and is ridiculously fun and full of energy.

Warm the Water: Show Me The Money (pg. 90)
Show Me The Money uses fake money as an opportunity to set financial goals.

Swim: Pitfall (pg. 75)
Pitfall explains how avoiding emergencies and wasteful opportunities can lead to building resources - especially money.

Towel Off: You Get a Prize (pg. 102)
This activity utilizes the great materials TRiO gives to its participants. Instead of just handing out backpacks, pens, or notebooks, reward the students who engage.

"Life is a state of consciousness." - Emmett Fox

Non-Verbal Speech

Workshop Title:
Non-Verbal Communication - What Does Your Body Language Say About You?

Workshop Category: Life Skills
Number of Participants: 10-20
Length of Workshop: 60 minutes
Space Required: Classroom
Props Needed: Index Cards, Writing Utensils, Paper, Markers, Tape

Activities:
Break the Ice: Web of Names (pg. 101)
Web of Names is an easy group initiative that focuses on learning the names of the people in the group.

Warm the Water: Draw Yourself (pg. 41)
Participants draw a picture of themselves achieving their greatest goal so that the group can learn more about each other.

Swim: Design by 3 (pg. 32)
The group must try to pass along a symbol or shape from the back of the line to the front of the line without looking at the original image.

Towel Off: Saying Goodbye (pg. 89)
Saying Goodbye is a very simple way for your group to anonymously post nice comments about other participants.

"When you cease to dream you cease to live." - Malcolm S. Forbes

Planning Dreams

Workshop Title:
Planning Dreams - How to Take the Action Steps Necessary to Discover Your Dreams

Workshop Category: Life Skills
Number of Participants: 10-20
Length of Workshop: 60 minutes
Space Required: Open Space
Props Needed: Paper Plates, Ropes, Throwables, Buckets

Activities:
Break the Ice: Hey You! (pg. 58)
Names are important, but sometimes it is hard to remember everyone in a large group. This is a non-threatening way to learn names.

Warm the Water: Dream Catcher (pg. 43)
This activity is meant to help your participants discover and develop their dreams and goals. Dream Catcher is based on the SMART goals theory.

Swim: Plan That Mine (pg. 78)
Planning is an important part of the college-going process. This activity expresses how to use your resources to accomplish the steps necessary to succeed.

Towel Off: Head, Heart, Hands (pg. 57)
We are sometimes guided by our head, sometimes guided by our heart, and sometime our hands. Use this check-in to see which part has been impacted.

"Reality leaves a lot to the imagination." - John Lennon

SMART Goals

Workshop Title:
SMART Goals - Turn Your Average Goals into SMART Goals

Workshop Category: High School Success/College Planning
Number of Participants: 5-50
Length of Workshop: 60 minutes
Space Required: Open Space
Props Needed: Bucket, Butcher Paper, Throwables, Markers, Paper, Writing Utensils

Activities:
Break the Ice: Gallery Walk (pg. 53)
Gallery Walks are a great way to create a small gallery around the room so the group can share ideas after an activity or before an event.

Warm the Water: Dream Catcher (pg. 43)
This activity is meant to help your participants discover and develop their dreams and goals. Dream Catcher is based on the SMART goals theory.

Swim: SMART Goal Paper Fold (pg. 91)
This activity will help participants make their goals more specific, measurable, attainable, relevant, and time-bound.

Towel Off: Gallery Walk (pg. 53)
Place questions at the top of the chart to process the group after the end of an activity.

"I have nothing to offer but blood, toil, tears, and sweat." Churchill

Time Management

Workshop Title:

Time Management - How to Take Back Your Time, Live in Quadrant 2, and Pursue the Career You Love

Workshop Category: Career Planning
Number of Participants: 5-50
Length of Workshop: 90 minutes
Space Required: Classroom
Props Needed: Butcher Paper, Joboo Cards, Careeragories Worksheets, Quadrants Handouts, Throwables

Activities:

Break the Ice: Careeragories (pg. 24)
In large groups, use this as an activity to learn names. Give more time but allow players to find names that start with the letter.

Warm the Water: Joboo (pg. 61)
Job-oo is based off of the classic board game Taboo. Instead of the group guessing random words like in Taboo, the group will try to guess careers.

Swim: Quadrants (pg. 86)
Quadrants is an interactive time-management activity that shows students how to prioritize their time.

Towel Off: Take a Stand (pg. 97)
Take A Stand debrief utilizes props to create conversations about an activity, initiative, or even at the end of a day.

"Failure is the path of least persistence." - Unknown

Trust Your Strengths

Workshop Title:
Trust Your Strengths - How to Use Your Strengths to Achieve a Goal With Your Team

Workshop Category: Life Skills
Number of Participants: 5-50
Length of Workshop: 60 minutes
Space Required: Open Space
Props Needed: Throwables, Blindfolds, Bucket, Index Cards, Writing Utensils,

Activities:
Break the Ice: Pit (pg. 73)
Give each participant nine index cards and ask them to write their top strength on all nine cards.

Warm the Water: Take a Stand (pg. 97)
Place items around the room and ask questions pertaining to the props. For example: Grab a stapler, a tape dispenser, and an eraser. Ask the participants to stand next to the item that describes their work ethic.

Swim: Snakes (pg. 94)
Snakes is a trust activity that focuses on non-verbal communication and how messages can get lost while going from person to person.

Towel Off: Likert Scale (pg. 68)
There are times before, during, or after an activity when the facilitator needs to check in with the group and Likert Scale fulfills that need.

"Live with passion." - Anthony Robbins

Paradigm Shift

Paradigm Shift offers leadership training and development with a primary focus to create opportunities for leaders to lead intentionally.

The Paradigm Shift consultants use practical leadership & adventure-based models to help leaders develop powerful relationships, set SMART goals, create personal responsibility, and develop a defined purpose.

We invite our participants to learn through dynamic keynotes, interactive workshops, online coaching, and customized training. Most importantly, Paradigm Shift will challenge your team to develop into leaders.

Find Paradigm Shift online at :

www.myparadigmshift.org

"Live life abundantly and with passion." - Kyle Price

Leadership Camps

PARADIGM SHIFT LEADERSHIP CAMPS

Paradigm Shift will change the way you do camps. An exciting trend for educational and faith-based organizations is hosting a leadership camp for students. These camps incorporate a variety of aspects of your program, and have drastically increased student engagement.

Camps can be 1-5 days and held during summer break, spring break, or even a weekend. Paradigm Shift specializes in designing every aspect of these incredible camps. Each camp will be focused on your program's objectives and desires.

Workshops

Each workshop is custom designed to work with your program's desired goals in mind. All workshops incorporate experiential learning (learning through a reflection of doing) and provide groups of all experience levels opportunities to create and enhance their leadership skills.

Our leadership workshops focus on strengths-based learning to cultivate powerful results. The Paradigm Shift staff creates every workshop based on your current curriculum, props and staff to develop an individualized event perfect your program!

Keynotes

PARADIGM SHIFT
KEYNOTES

The Paradigm Shift team treats their keynotes as more than a lecture. It is a conversation. It is powerful. It is fun. More than anything, it is an opportunity for the audience to become engaged in the leadership material they are learning and to make it applicable to their own lives.

We use cutting edge theories and techniques from experiential-based learning to infuse leadership into every single one of our keynote addresses. We invite the audience to join us on an adventure of learning in a fresh and challenging way.

Coaching

Would you like individual advice and coaching on how to lead your groups? Paradigm Shift offers individual consulting for trainers who want to take the next step in their facilitation.

Each participant enrolled in the coaching classes will also be involved in an online mastermind group that includes many of the best trainers from around the world. We will look at your programming to fine-tune your skills, update your curriculum, & provide you with individualized opportunities for leadership development.

Train the Trainer

Paradigm Shift specializes in training group leaders who want to make a better connections with their participants. In these specialized trainings, our facilitators will walk you through the steps necessary to create better engagement, promote more powerful relationships, and allow substantial change to occur with a group.

Our curriculum has been proven through years of experience with thousands of groups. We follow the "Pool Party Process," a model that prepares groups to experience incredible learning. These trainings are interactive, engaging and customizable to your program

emotiCARDS

EmotiCards were created for educators, counselors, group leaders, and all individuals who need a creative way to explain emotions to their group.

These cards invite participants to engage in conversation about their emotions, feelings, or experiences. Leaders can use these cards in a multitude of ways – as a processing tool, an icebreaker, leadership initiative, or for just plain fun.

A pack of EmotiCARDS costs $10.

You can order EmotiCARDS for your group on the Paradigm Shift website:

www.myparadigmshift.org/emoticards

emotiCARDS
Activity Guide

The activities in this book take full advantage of the fun, yet powerful emotions that are displayed on EmotiCARDS.

Group leaders of all skill levels and experiences can use EmotiCARDS to promote two separate areas of learning...discovering emotions and processing emotions.

The EmotiCARDS Activity Guide has 20 brand new activities, variations for any group, and lists of 200+ emotions.

The EmotiCARDS Activity Guide costs $15.

You can order the EmotiCARDS Activity Guide for your group on the Paradigm Shift website:

www.myparadigmshift.org/emoticards

Authors

Ryan Eller

Ryan is the founder and lead consultant of Paradigm Shift, which provides custom-built team-building and leadership training. Ryan has facilitated in 30 US states and hosted leadership conferences in Cuba, Brazil, and Australia. Ryan has the goal of hosting a leadership training in all 50 states and all 7 continents.

Ryan received his Bachelor's Degree in Mass Communication and Master's Degree in Higher Education Administration from Northeastern State University. He is a member of ODSA, SWASAP, and COE. He loves nothing more than a great Nick Collison pick while eating brinner with his beautiful wife Kristin and his little princess Jane.

Jerrod Murr

Murr has been speaking to groups since he was 14. He really stepped up his game in his early twenties. Murr works with small groups in experiential learning settings, as well as keynotes to groups in the thousands. A few speaking highlights include the privilege of planning a leadership conference for over 300 pastors in Cuba, speaking to over 1,000 students in Brazil, and holding the microphone for his kindergarten class song.

Murr currently serves as the Director of 20 Camps and Leadership Develop for Paradigm Shift. He resides in Muskogee, OK with his wife, Jenn, daughter Adelae, and Josalyn. His favorite book is The Giving Tree, and he loves basketball, the OKC Thunder, and good coffee.

Notes

_____

_____

_____

_____

_____

_____

_____

_____

_____

_____

_____

_____

_____

_____

_____

_____

Notes

_____

_____

_____

_____

_____

_____

_____

_____

_____

_____

_____

_____

_____

_____

_____

_____

_____

_____

Notes

Notes

_____

_____

_____

_____

_____

_____

_____

_____

_____

_____

_____

_____

_____

_____

_____

_____

_____

_____

Notes

30998774R10076

Made in the USA
San Bernardino, CA
29 February 2016